KU-167-684

Six Thinking Hats

EDWARD DE BONO

VIKING

VIKING

Penguin Books Ltd, Harmondsworth, Middlesex, England
Viking Penguin Inc., 40 West 23rd Street, New York, New York 10010, U.S.A.
Penguin Books Australia Ltd, Ringwood, Victoria, Australia
Penguin Books Canada Limited, 2801 John Street, Markham, Ontario, Canada L3R 1B4
Penguin Books (N.Z.) Ltd, 182–190 Wairau Road, Auckland 10, New Zealand

First published in Canada by Key Porter Books Ltd 1985
First published in Great Britain by Viking 1986

Copyright © Mica Management Resources Inc., 1985

All rights reserved
Without limiting the rights under copyright
reserved above, no part of this publication may be
reproduced, stored in or introduced into a retrieval system,
or transmitted, in any form or by any means (electronic, mechanical,
photocopying, recording or otherwise), without the prior
written permission of both the copyright owner and
the above publisher of this book

Printed and bound in Great Britain
by William Clowes Limited,
Beccles and London

British Library Cataloguing in Publication Data

De Bono, Edward
Six thinking hats.
1. Reasoning
I. Title
160   BC177

ISBN 0–670–81314–1

Contents

Preface

Can you really change the effectiveness of your thinking?

In January 1985 *Time* magazine chose as "Man of the Year" the person who was ultimately responsible for the superbly successful Los Angeles Olympic Games: Peter Ueberroth. The usual pattern of such games is that they lose hundreds of millions of dollars. Even though the city of Los Angeles had voted not to spend any municipal funds on the games, the 1984 Olympics actually made a surplus of $250 million. The extra-ordinary success of the games depended heavily on new concepts and new ideas, which were put into practice with leadership and efficiency.

What sort of thinking was needed to generate these new concepts?

In an interview in the *Washington Post* on September 30, 1984, Peter Ueberroth explains how he used lateral thinking to generate new concepts. Lateral thinking is a technique which I developed many years ago. I have written many books about it. Peter Ueberroth had come to a one-hour talk I had been invited to give to the Young Presidents' Organisation *nine years previously.*

There are hundreds of other examples of how a deliberate thinking technique has had a powerful impact. I can only design the techniques and put them forward. It is up to individuals like Mr. Ueberroth to pick up on the techniques and to put them to work.

Thinking is the ultimate human resource. Yet we can never be satisfied with our most important skill. No matter how good we become, we should always want to be better. Usually, the only people who are very satisfied with their thinking skill are those poor thinkers who believe that the purpose of thinking is to prove yourself right – to your own satisfaction. If we have only a limited view of what thinking can do, we may be smug about our excellence in this area, but not otherwise.

The main difficulty of thinking is confusion. We try to do too much at once. Emotions, information, logic, hope and creativity all crowd in on us. It is like juggling with too many balls.

What I am putting forward in this book is a very simple concept which allows a thinker to do one thing at a time. He or she becomes able to separate emotion from logic, creativity from information, and so on. The concept is that of the six thinking hats. Putting on any one of these hats defines a certain type of thinking. In the book I describe the nature and contribution of each type of thinking.

The six thinking hats allow us to conduct our thinking as a conductor might lead an orchestra. We can call forth what we will. Similarly, in any meeting it is very useful to switch people out of their usual track in order to get them to think differently about the matter at hand.

It is the sheer *convenience* of the six thinking hats that is the main value of the concept.

E.B.

CHAPTER 1

Playacting
IF YOU PLAYACT BEING A THINKER
YOU WILL BECOME ONE

I believe that one of the two Rodin originals for *The Thinker* is in Buenos Aires in the square in front of the parliament building. At least that is what my guide told me as she pointed to this busy thinker frozen into immortal bronze.

As a *fact* this may well be wrong on several counts. It may not be an original. There may not have been two originals. My guide might have been mistaken. It may not be in the square in front of the parliament building. My memory might be mistaken. So why should I put forward something which has not been checked out absolutely as a fact? There are many reasons.

One reason is that later in this book I shall refer specifically to the use of facts. Another reason is to provoke those people who feel that facts are more important than their use. Another reason is that I want the reader to visualize that famous thinker figure, wherever it may be. The real reason is that this book was written in an airplane on a journey from London to Kuala Lumpur in Malaysia. In any case I did use the words "I believe," which indicate my state of belief rather than a dogmatically asserted fact. We often need to indicate *the way in which something is being put forward*. That is what this book is all about.

I want you to imagine that much used – and over-used – image of Rodin's *The Thinker*. I want you to imagine that chin-on-hand pose which is supposed to come to any thinker who is being more than just frivolous. As a matter of fact, I believe that thinking should be active and brisk rather than gloomy and solemn. But the traditional image is a useful one for the moment.

Throw yourself into that pose – physically not mentally – and you will become a thinker. Why? Because if you playact being a thinker, you will become one.

The Tibetans say prayers by revolving their prayer wheels on which the prayers are inscribed. The rotating wheels spiral the prayers into divine space. Indeed, if the wheels are properly balanced, one assistant can keep a dozen prayer wheels turning like the circus act in which whirling plates are balanced on top of long sticks. It may be that the Tibetan is allowed to think of his laundry list while he spins the wheel. It is the intention to pray that counts rather than the emotional or spiritual flutterings that many Christians demand of themselves. There is another Christian view that is much closer to the Tibetan: go through the motions of praying even if you do not feel emotionally involved. In time your emotions will catch up with your motions. That is precisely what I mean by asking you to playact being a thinker.

Adopt the pose of a thinker. Go through the motions. Have the intention and make it manifest to yourself and to those around. Quite soon your brain will follow the role you are playing. If you playact being a thinker, you will indeed become one. This book sets out the different *roles* for your playacting.

CHAPTER 2

Putting on a Hat
A VERY DELIBERATE PROCESS

The most striking feature of any crowd photograph taken more than forty years ago is that *everyone* is wearing a hat. Newspaper photographs and early films show this tremendous prevalence of hats.

Today a hat is a rarity, especially among men. Today hats tend to define a role. Hats are used as part of a uniform, which itself defines a role.

A bossy husband who issues orders to his family may be said to be wearing his "headmaster's hat" or his "chief executive hat." An executive may distinguish between the two roles she plays by telling her audience that she is wearing "an executive hat" or a "housewife hat." Mrs. Thatcher, the prime minister of England, occasionally claims that she carries over the prudence and frugality of a housewife into the management of government.

Just as well established is the idea of a *thinking hat* or a *thinking cap.*

. . . I'll have to put on my thinking hat and consider your new proposal. I am not sure I want to sell that building.

. . . Put on your thinking cap and phone me tomorrow.

. . . This is a dangerous development. We'll have to put on our thinking hats to see how we can get out of this mess.

I have always imagined the thinking hat as a sort of floppy nightcap with a tassle. Rather like a dunce's cap but without the stiff arrogance that is the only real hallmark of stupidity.

People volunteer to put on their own thinking hats or they request others to do so.

The deliberate *putting on* of a hat is something very definite.

In bygone days when Nanny put on her hat it was a definite signal that she – and the children – were going out. There was to be no argument. The signal was final. When a policeman puts on his hat, duty and performance are clearly signaled. Soldiers without hats never seem quite as serious or frightening as soldiers with hats.

It is a pity there is not a genuine thinking hat that you could buy in a store. In Germany and Denmark there is a student hat, which is a sort of scholar's cap. But scholarship and thinking are rarely the same thing. Scholars are too busy learning about the thinking of others to do any thinking for themselves.

Consider the usefulness of a *real thinker's hat.*

. . . Don't disturb me. Can't you see I am thinking?

. . . I am going to break off this discussion so that we can all put on our thinking hats and do some focused thinking on this matter.

. . . I want you to think about this right now. Let me see you put on your thinking hat.

. . . I want you to have second thoughts on this plan. Put your thinking hat back on your head.

. . . You pay me to think. So here I am sitting thinking. The better you pay, the better I think.

. . . How about giving this some deliberate thought? Up to now you have just given me knee-jerk reactions. Put on your thinking hat.

. . . Thinking is not an excuse for inaction but a way to get better action. So let's have the action.

That mental picture of someone wearing a real thinking hat could serve to switch on the tranquil and detached state of mind needed for any thinking that is to be more than mere reacting to a situation. Perhaps conscientious thinkers could set aside five minutes of the day for a deliberate wearing of the thinking hat. It depends on whether you believe you are paid to think or to follow the thinking of others.

I want to focus on the matter of *deliberate thinking.* That is the purpose of the thinking hat. You put it on in a deliberate manner.

There is the walking-talking-breathing type of thinking that we do all the time. We answer the telephone. We cross the road. We switch in and out of routines. We do not need to be conscious of which leg follows which when we walk or of how to manage our breathing. There is a constant background of this type of ongoing automatic thinking. But there is a different sort of thinking that is much more deliberate and focused. Background thinking is for routine *coping.* Deliberate thinking is for doing better than just coping. Everyone can run, but an athlete runs deliberately and is trained for that purpose.

There is no easy way of signaling to ourselves that we want to switch out of this routine, coping type of thinking and into the deliberate type. So the thinking hat idiom becomes a definite signal we can give to ourselves or to others.

Let us contrast these two types of thinking: coping and deliberate.

When you are driving a car, you have to choose roads and follow roads and keep out of the way of other traffic. There is a lot of moment to moment activity dictated by the last moment and by the next moment. You are looking for signals and reacting to them. This is *reactive thinking.* So the walking-talking-breathing type of thinking is very like driving along a road. You read signposts and make decisions. But you do not *make the map.*

The other type of thinking has to do with *mapmaking.* You explore the subject and make the map. You make the map in an objective and neutral fashion. To do this you must look broadly. This is quite different from just reacting to signposts as they appear.

This contrast is shown in the following example.

Imagine that you are trying to win an argument. You put forward your case and summon up all the points in favor of that case. You listen to your opponent's case only to attack it and to expose its weaknesses. Moment to moment you are attacking or defending. Each side reacts to the other side.

Contrast a mapmaking procedure.

I run a program for the teaching of thinking in schools. It is called the CoRT (Cognitive Research Trust) program and is now used by several million school-children in different countries. The first lesson is called the PMI. Instead of just *reacting* to a situation, the youngster makes a simple map. He or she does this by looking first in the "Plus" direction and noting down what is observed. Then the youngster looks in the "Minus" direction, and finally in the "Interesting" direction (for all those things which are worth noting but do not fit under either "Plus" or "Minus"). The map is now made. The thinker chooses his or her route.

One girl put it very neatly. She said: "I thought doing a PMI was silly and artificial because I knew what I thought. But when I had done the PMI, I found that my mind was changed by what I, myself, had written down."

It is a matter of directing attention and of having a way to do that.

In Sydney, Australia, a class of thirty young boys all voted in favor of receiving $5 a week for going to school. After doing a PMI and without any prompting from the teacher, twenty-nine of the boys changed their minds and decided that it was not a good idea.

A businessman who had been arguing for months with a major oil company asked everyone to do a PMI at their next meeting. He told me that the problem was solved in twenty minutes. Once the "map" had been laid out, a route could be chosen.

A woman who had planned for two years to move from California to Arizona did a PMI with her two sons. At the end of the brief exercise the move was canceled.

One of the world's greatest inventors, Paul MacCready (the inventor of man-powered flight), was caught up in a bureaucratic problem. His son suggested he do a PMI and this provided the next move.

The mapmaking type of thinking requires a certain detachment. The walking-talking-breathing type of thinking does not. Indeed, this reactive type of thinking can only function when there is something to react against. That is why the notion of critical thinking as the complete form of thinking can be very dangerous. There is a silly belief, based on misinterpretation of the Greek master thinkers, that thinking is based on dialogue and dialectical argument. This belief has done much harm to Western thinking.

The Western habit of argument and dialectic is defective because it leaves out the generative and creative. Critical thinking is fine for reacting to what is put before you, but does nothing to produce proposals.

Pupils in school are very concerned with reacting to what is put before them: textbook material, teachers' comments, TV series, etc. But as soon as a youngster leaves school, he or she will have to do much more than just react. There will need to be initiative and plans and action. These are not going to come from reactive thinking.

To cover this "action thinking," I invented the term *operacy*. This is the skill of doing – and the thinking that goes with it. The word *operacy* is designed to sound like literacy and numeracy because I strongly believe that operacy should rank alongside literacy and numeracy as a basic ingredient in education. Indeed, the CoRT thinking lessons are concerned with operacy thinking: setting goals, assessing priorities, generating alternatives, etc.

If we are not merely to react to what is in front of us, then we must have a way of directing attention. The PMI is one of the CoRT ways of doing this. In this book we look at another way.

When a color map is printed, the colors are separated. First one color is put onto the paper. Then a second color is overprinted. Then the next and so on until a full-color map comes out at the end.

In this book the six thinking hats correspond to the different colors used in printing a map. That is the method I intend to use for directing attention. So it is not only a matter of putting on a thinking hat but also of choosing what *color* thinking hat you are going to use.

CHAPTER 3

Intention and Performance

I want to get back to the distinction between *intention* and *performance* because so many people have the wrong view of this matter.

I have said that if you go through the motions of being a thinker – for example, putting on your thinking hat – then eventually you will become a thinker. Your thinking will follow the motions. Your playacting will become real.

I seem to be claiming that if you have the intention of becoming a thinker, your performance will follow.

Many people will rush to point out the absurdity of this. So let me do it for them. If you have the intention of becoming a weightlifter, will this intention suffice to raise the weights? If you have the intention of becoming a chess player, will this move the pieces expertly around the board? The answer is no, because in these cases we are looking for exceptional performance.

But if you have the intention of becoming a cook, and you go through the motions, then you will become a tolerable cook. You will not become an Escoffier unless you have the needed talent, but you *will* be much more of a cook than someone who has not had the intention and has not gone through the motions.

Please note that the intention is not enough. *You must go through the motions.* It is not enough for a Tibetan to have the intention of saying prayers: he must rotate the prayer wheel.

It is certainly not enough for the thinker to consider himself or herself to be a thinker. That is almost the exact *opposite* of what I am saying. If you already consider yourself to be a thinker, then you are likely to do nothing about it – because you are smug and satisfied with your assumed skill.

I once asked a group of very well educated Americans (graduate school) to give themselves a mark, out of ten, for their thinking ability. To my astonishment the average mark was eight out of ten. In other words, their horizons of what thinking could do were so limited that each person reckoned his or her thinking was almost as good as it could possibly be. To be more charitable, I suppose many of the audience probably misunderstood the question. They knew that they had always been in the top ten percent at school and at university so the mark of eight was a modest acknowledgment of this comparative performance. I was, of course, looking for an absolute rating. Nevertheless, people are remarkably complacent about their thinking – because they cannot conceive how it might be improved.

The intention to become a thinker is very important because it is so rare. I do not recall ever meeting anyone who actually wanted to become a thinker. This should be no surprise in view of what I have written above. Besides, wanting to become a thinker implies that you are not one already. Humor, sex and thinking are all activities at which everyone knows himself or herself to be competent.

When Dr. Luis Alberto Machado asked to be made Minister for the Development of Intelligence in the Venezuelan government, there were hoots of laughter all around. But he persisted and eventually 106,000 teachers were trained in the use of the CoRT thinking lessons. By law, every schoolchild in Venezuela must spend two hours a week specifically developing thinking skills. There are lessons called "thinking." Pupils know this, so do teachers and educators, so do parents.

The actual thinking skills that the pupils acquire are important. But far more important is the idea of *developing thinking skills*. The usual self-image of a youngster at school is that he or she is "intelligent" or "not intelligent" depending on how well he or she gets along at school and pleases the teacher. This concept of intelligence is a value concept. It is like being short or tall, beautiful or plain. There is not much you can do about it.

Being a thinker is a totally different self-image. It is an *operating skill*. You can do something about it. You can get better at thinking just as you can get better at playing football or cooking. The Venezuelan youngsters know that they can set out to think about something and they know that they will come up with some ideas. For this they use the CoRT frameworks.

Using the thinking hats described in this book is one
way of reinforcing that *intention* to be a thinker.

Being a thinker does not involve being right all the
time. Indeed, anyone who is right all the time is likely
to be a poor thinker (arrogant, uninterested in exploration, unable to see alternatives, etc.). Being a thinker
does not involve being clever. Nor does it involve
solving all those cunning problems that people always
expect me to solve. Being a thinker involves consciously wanting to be a thinker. This is much simpler
than being a golfer, a tennis player or a musician.
There is less equipment involved for one thing.

So *intention* is the first step. It is both easy and
difficult at the same time. Not unlike those Zen habits
which are easy to write about but not so easy to do.
That is why there is a need for some tangible structures
– the six thinking hats.

Now we can look at the *performance* aspect. Does a
furrowed brow and chin on hand really make a
difference? The answer is yes if it is deliberate and no
if it is natural. The surprising thing is that on a
physiological level it might actually work. There is
some evidence to suggest that if you assume a smile
then your physiology follows and you become happier
and less able to be angry. People react to artificially
smiling models in advertisements as if their smiles
were real. Signals become reality. The mask is followed
by the substance.

On a more basic level, if you *intend* to listen to the
other person, then you will spend somewhat more time
listening – and your thinking will improve. If you
consciously wrinkle your brow to think, you will not

make a decision until you unwrinkle your brow and that should produce a better decision than the off-the-cuff one. Violent youngsters taught thinking became less violent because they did not have to snap immediately into a violent clichéd reaction.

The six thinking hats provide a tangible way of translating intention into performance.

CHAPTER 4

Role-playing
AN EGO HOLIDAY

People do not mind "playing the fool" so long as it is quite clear that they are just playing a role. They even take pride in putting on a good performance and playing an extremely foolish fool. That now becomes a measure of achievement and excellence. The role has taken over and the ego is now the stage director.

One of the problems with Zen Buddhism is that the harder the ego tries "not-to-be-there," the more present it becomes in its "trying." One style of actor loses his or her ego identity and takes on the ego of the role (method acting). Another style of actor directs his or her own performance. Both are good actors. Both are having an ego holiday. One is having a holiday abroad and the other is having a holiday at home.

To play at being someone else allows the ego to go beyond its normal restrictive self-image. Actors are often quite shy in ordinary life. But a role gives freedom. We might have difficulty in seeing ourselves being foolish, wrong or outsmarted. Given a well-defined role we can act out such parts with pleasure in our acting skill rather than damage to our egos. There is prestige in being considered a good actor.

Without the protection of a formal role, the ego is at risk. That is why habitually negative people claim the role of devil's advocate when they want to be negative. This means to imply that they are not normally negative, but that it is useful to have someone play this role and that they intend to play it well. This traditional role of devil's advocate is very similar to the black thinking hat that will be described later. But instead of just one thinking role there are going to be six, each one defined by a different thinking hat.

To role-play being a thinker in the general sense of that word is a valuable step towards becoming a thinker. But we can go further by breaking down that large role into more specific parts. These become character parts like the character parts in a good pantomime, a good TV soap opera or a traditional Western movie. Or in a very pure form in the Japanese Kabuki theater where the roles are highly stylized.

Everyone can recognize the witch in a pantomime. She cackles and gloats and enjoys being hissed and booed by the audience. That is her role and she plays it to the full. Then there is the noble prince who represents the forces of good. Ordinary humanity is represented by the dame. By tradition the prince is played by a girl and the dame by a man. This makes a lot of sense because the whole purpose of pantomime roles is to get as far away from reality as possible in order to illustrate ideas. Real-life roles would only illustrate themselves. Pantomime roles are designed to represent grand forces that become humanized for our amusement. So the more deliberate and artificial the role, the more it becomes recognizable as a role. That is the secret of success of American TV soap operas; that is why JR in "Dallas" is lovable.

The broad thinking hat role is broken down into six different *character roles*, represented by six differently colored thinking hats.

You choose which of the six hats to put on at any one moment. You put on that hat and then play the role defined by that hat. You watch yourself playing that role. You play the role as well as you can. Your ego is protected by the role. Your ego is involved in playing the role well.

When you change thinking hats you have to change roles. Each role should be distinct. As distinct as the witch and the prince in a pantomime. You become a bunch of different thinkers – all using the same head.

All this is part of the mapmaking type of thinking. As I have said, each colored hat represents a different color that might be used in the printing of a map. At the end the colors come together to give the completed map.

Each of the six thinking hats is described in the following pages. They are meant to be as different and distinct as possible. They should be worn that way. The red hat is quite different from the white hat. The yellow hat and the black hat are in sharp contrast. The blue hat role is distinct from the green hat role.

Playing comedy is not playing tragedy. When you are wearing the clown's costume, then play the clown. When you wear the villain's hat, play the villain. Take pride in playing the different parts.

Thinking now begins to flow from the *acted parts* and not from your *ego*. That is how maps are made. Then, in the end, the ego can choose a preferred route.

CHAPTER 5

Melancholy and Other Fluids

This chapter is designed for those who are still not convinced. It is for those who still feel that the concept of six different thinking hats is a frivolous and pointless game which can add nothing to our thinking skills. Such people should read this chapter. Others may skip it if they so wish.

Perhaps the Greeks were right to believe that different body fluids affected their moods. If you were gloomy and melancholic, that was because a "black bile" flowed through your system. In fact, the word *melancholy* means just that: "black bile." So your mood was determined by the fluids or "humors" that pervaded your system at the moment. Such fluids affected your mood and your mood affected your thinking.

Many depressed people have noticed that the thoughts they are capable of thinking while they are depressed are quite different from the thoughts they can think when in a more cheerful frame of mind.

Because we now know so much more about the brain, we can make a good case for the Greek fluids. We know that the balance of chemicals (neurotransmitters) acting in the hypothalamus can strongly affect behavior. We know about endorphins, which are morphine-like chemicals released within the brain (giving joggers their "high"). We know that complex neuropeptides released from the pituitary gland can travel elsewhere in the brain and be broken down into specific chemicals that affect different parts of the brain. We suspect that spring fever in animals is caused in this way (the changing balance of light and dark causes the pituitary to release chemicals that activate sexual interest). In time we may learn how chemicals in the brain – and possibly in the general bloodstream – have a marked affect on our mood and on our thinking.

It is also very well established that physiological responses can be altered through the normal processes of conditioning, as Pavlov showed. Animals have been trained to raise or lower their blood pressure in response to an external signal.

It is possible that the six distinct thinking hats can, over time, acquire the status of a conditioning signal that triggers a particular chemical background in the brain and that in turn will affect our thinking.

We can approach this matter from quite a different point of view and get the same result.

If we look at the brain as an *active* information system, we find that its behavior is quite different from that of the *passive* information systems used in computers and elsewhere (printing, for example). I described active systems, in a preliminary sort of way, in *The Mechan-*

ism of Mind. This book was published in 1969 and is only now being discovered by Fifth Generation computer scientists who have come round to the view that self-organizing active systems are essential.

An active system means that the information organizes itself into patterns instead of lying passively on a surface waiting for some outside processor to organize it.

A tray contains sand. A steel ball dropped onto the surface stays where it has fallen. If the ball is dropped through a particular square in a grid, it remains directly under that square. This is a passive information system. The ball stays where it has been placed.

Another tray contains a floppy latex rubber bag filled with a very viscous oil. The first ball dropped onto the surface gradually sinks to the bottom, pushing the surface of the rubber bag before it. When the ball comes to rest, there is now a contour in the surface, a sort of depression at the bottom of which rests the first ball. A second ball rolls down the gradient and comes to rest against the first ball. The second ball is active. It does not stay where it has been put but follows the gradient created by the first ball. In fact, all subsequent balls will roll towards the first ball and a cluster will form. So here we have a simple active surface which allows the incoming information (the balls) to organize itself into a cluster.

These are very primitive models, but they serve to illustrate the vast difference between passive systems and active systems. It is unfortunate that all our thinking has been about passive systems because the universe of active information systems is totally different.

It is possible to show how nerve networks behave as active self-organizing information systems and that is what I set out to do in *The Mechanism of Mind*. As a matter of fact, the model I put forward in the book has now been simulated on computer and does perform largely as predicted.

It is the active nature of nerve networks that allows incoming information to organize itself into patterns. It is the formation and the use of such patterns that give rise to *perception*. Were it not for this ability of the brain to allow incoming information to organize itself into patterns, then even such simple things as crossing the road would be virtually impossible.

Our brains are designed to be brilliantly uncreative. They are designed to form patterns and then to use such fixed patterns on every possible occasion in the future.

But self-organizing systems do have one great disadvantage. They remain imprisoned by the sequence of their experience (this history of happenings). That is why Fifth Generation computers will need to be equipped with humor, emotions or the ability to make silly mistakes. Otherwise they can never think.

The thresholds and sensitivities of the nerve units are much altered by the bathing chemicals. A change in these chemicals results in the stabilizing of a different pattern. In a sense we have a *different brain* for each different chemical background.

This suggests that emotions are an essential part of our thinking ability and not just something extra that mucks up our thinking.

People who have difficulty making decisions might reflect that different chemical settings of the brain have each made a decision that is right for that particular setting. So both choices are right – but for different brains. Hence the indecision.

In times of panic or anger people tend to behave in a primitive manner. This may be because the brain is so rarely under these special chemical conditions that there has been no chance to acquire complex reaction patterns. This would mean that there is a very good reason for training people under such emotional conditions (as the military have always done).

So we see the importance of changed chemical settings in the brain. On the one hand this arises from our increasing knowledge about brain behavior. On the other hand it arises from theoretical considerations of the behavior of active self-organizing information systems.

What has this to do with the six thinking hats?

I mentioned earlier that these hats could become conditioning triggers, which could, conceivably, alter chemical balances in the brain. The unscrambling of the different aspects of thinking is also very important. If we set out to think in the normal way, we either try to exclude emotions (which then continue to play a highly influential hidden role in the background) or we zigzag between reason and emotion. If there are indeed different chemical settings associated with different modes of thinking, then this scrambled type of thinking never gives the brain a chance to establish any setting.

CHAPTER 6

The Purpose of Six Hat Thinking

The first value of the six thinking hats is that of defined *role-playing*. The main restriction on thinking is ego defence, which is responsible for most of the practical faults of thinking. The hats allow us to think and say things that we could not otherwise think and say without risking our egos. Wearing the clown costume gives you full permission to play the clown.

The second value is that of *attention directing*. If our thinking is to be more than just reactive, then we must have a way of directing attention to one aspect after another. The six hats give us a means for directing attention to six different aspects of the matter.

The third value is that of *convenience*. The symbolism of the six different hats provides a very convenient way of asking someone (including yourself) to switch gears. You can ask someone to be negative or to stop being negative. You can ask someone to be creative. You can ask someone to give his or her purely emotional response.

The fourth value is the *possible basis in brain chemistry*, which I outlined in the previous chapter. I am prepared to make claims that go somewhat beyond our present state of knowledge because the theoretical demands of self-organizing systems justify such extrapolation.

The fifth value arises from establishing the *rules of the game*. People are very good at learning the rules of the game. Learning the rules of the game is one of the most powerful forms of learning in children, which is why they are so adept at using computers. The six thinking hats establish certain rules for the "game" of thinking. The particular game of thinking that I have in mind is mapmaking as distinct from argument.

CHAPTER 7

Six Hats, Six Colors

Each of the six thinking hats has a color: white, red, black, yellow, green, blue. The color provides the name for the hat.

I could have chosen clever Greek names to indicate the type of thinking required by each hat. That would have been impressive and would have pleased some people. But it would be of little practical value since the names would be difficult to remember.

I want thinkers to *visualize* and to imagine the hats as actual hats. For this to happen color is important. How else could you distinguish between the hats? Different shapes would again be difficult to learn and would be confusing. Color makes the imaging easier.

The color of each hat is also related to its function.

White Hat White is neutral and objective. The white hat is concerned with objective facts and figures.

Red Hat Red suggests anger (seeing red), rage and emotions. The red hat gives the emotional view.

Black Hat Black is gloomy and negative. The black hat covers the negative aspects – why it cannot be done.

Yellow Hat Yellow is sunny and positive. The yellow hat is optimistic and covers hope and positive thinking.

Green Hat Green is grass, vegetation and abundant, fertile growth. The green hat indicates creativity and new ideas.

Blue Hat Blue is cool, and it is also the color of the sky, which is above everything else. The blue hat is concerned with control and the organization of the thinking process. Also the use of the other hats.

Remembering the function of each hat is easy if you remember the color and the associations. The function of the hat will then follow. You may also think of them as three pairs:

White and red

Black and yellow

Green and blue.

In practice the hats are *always* referred to by their color and *never* by their function. There is a good reason for this. If you ask someone to give their emotional reaction to something, you are unlikely to get an honest answer because people think it is wrong to be emotional. But the term *red hat* is neutral. You can ask someone to "take off the black hat for a moment" more easily than you can ask that person to stop being so negative. The neutrality of the colors allows the hats to be used without embarrassment. Thinking becomes a game with defined rules rather than a matter of exhortation and condemnation.

The hats are referred to directly:

. . . I want you to take off your black hat.

. . . For a few moments let us all put on our red thinking hats.

. . . That's fine for yellow hat thinking. Now let's have the white hat.

When you are dealing with people who have not read this book and who are unaware of the symbolism of the six thinking hats, the explanation attached to each color can quickly give the flavor of each hat. You should then follow up by giving those people a copy of this book to read. The more widespread the idiom, the more efficient it will be in use. Eventually you should be able to sit down at any discussion table and switch in and out of "hats" with ease.

CHAPTER 8

The White Hat

FACTS AND FIGURES

Can you role-play being a computer?

Just give the facts in a neutral and objective manner.

Never mind the interpretation: just the facts please.

What are the facts in this matter?

Computers are not yet emotional (though we shall probably have to make them emotional if they are to think intelligently). We expect a computer to show us the facts and figures on demand. We do not expect a computer to argue with us and to use its facts and figures only in support of its argument.

Too often the facts and figures are embedded in an argument. The facts are used for some purpose rather than presented as facts. Facts and figures can never be treated objectively when put forward as part of an argument.

So we badly need a switch that says: "Just the facts please – without the argument."

Unfortunately, Western thinking with its argument habits, prefers to give a conclusion first and then to bring in the facts to support that conclusion. In contrast, in the mapmaking type of thinking that I am advocating, we have to make the map first and then choose the route. That means that we have to have the facts and figures first.

So white hat thinking is a convenient way of asking for the facts and figures to be put forward in a neutral and objective manner.

At one time a mammoth anti-trust case was being pursued against International Business Machines in the United States. The case was eventually dropped – probably because it was realized that the U.S. needed the strength of IBM in order to compete with the highly organized Japanese electronic competition. It has also been suggested that there was another reason for dropping the case. IBM provided so many documents (about seven million, I believe) that no court could cope with the volume. If the judge dies during the course of a case, the case has to start all over again. Since judges are not appointed until they are relatively old enough to be relatively wise, there was a very good chance of the judge dying in the course of the case. So the case was untriable unless a very young judge was appointed in order to make this case his or her whole career.

The point of this story is that it is possible to reply to a request for facts and figures with so much information that the asker is overwhelmed by the amount.

. . . If you want the facts and figures you can (expletive deleted) have them. All of them.

This sort of response is understandable because any attempt to simplify the facts could be seen as a selection of facts to make a particular case.

In order to avoid being drowned in information, the person requesting the white hat thinking can focus his or her request in order to draw forth the needed information.

. . . Give me your broad white hat thinking on unemployment.

. . . Now give me the figures for school-leavers six months after they have left school.

The framing of suitable focusing questions is part of the normal process of asking for information. Lawyers skilled in cross-examination do this all the time. Ideally, the witness should be wearing the white thinking hat and should answer the questions factually. Judges and courtroom lawyers might find the white hat idiom most convenient.

. . . As I said, he returned to his apartment at six-thirty in the morning because he had spent the whole night gambling.

. . . Mr. Jones, did you actually see the defendant gambling on the night of June 30, or did he tell you he had been gambling?

. . . No, Your Honor. But he goes gambling almost every night.

. . . Mr. Jones, if you were wearing the white thinking hat what might you have said?

... I observed the defendant return to his apartment at six-thirty in the morning on July 1.

... Thank you. You may step down.

It has to be said that lawyers in a courtroom are *always* trying to make a case. Their questions are therefore framed to support their line of argument or to destroy the line of argument of the other side. This is, of course, exactly the opposite of white hat thinking. The role of the judge is a curious one.

In the Dutch legal system there is no jury. The three judges or assessors try to use pure white hat thinking in order to find out the facts of the case. Their task is to make the "map" and then to pass judgement. This does not seem to be the case in England or the United States where the judge is there to preserve the rules of evidence and then to respond to the evidence extracted by the lawyers either directly or by means of a jury.

So any person framing questions in order to extract information needs to be sure that he or she is using the white thinking hat *himself or herself.* Are you really trying to get the facts or to build up a case for an idea forming in your head?

... Last year there was a twenty-five percent increase in the sale of turkey meat in the U.S., due to the interest in dieting and the concern with health. Turkey meat is perceived as being "lighter."

... Mr. Fitzler, I have asked you to put on your *white hat.* The fact is the twenty-five percent increase. The rest is your interpretation.

. . . No, sir. Market research clearly shows that the reason people give for buying turkey meat is that they think it is lower in cholesterol.

. . . Well then you have two facts. Fact one: that turkey meat sales have risen by twenty-five percent in the last year. Fact two: some market research shows that people claim to buy turkey meat because of their concern with cholesterol.

The white hat gives a sort of direction to aim towards in dealing with information. We can aim to play the white hat role as well as possible. This means aiming to get the pure facts. It is obvious that the white hat role involves some skill – perhaps more than the other hats.

. . . There is a rising trend in the number of women smoking cigars.

. . . That is not a fact.

. . . It is. I have the figures here.

. . . What your figures show is that for each of the last three years the number of women smoking cigars has risen above the level for the previous year.

. . . Isn't that a trend?

. . . It could be. But that is an interpretation. To me a trend suggests something that is happening and will continue to happen. The figures are the fact. It may be that women are smoking more cigars because they are smoking more anyway – possibly due to increased anxiety. Or it may simply be that over the last three years cigarmakers have spent an unusual amount of money persuading women to smoke cigars. The first is a trend that could provide opportunities. The second is much less of an opportunity.

. . . I simply used the word *trend* to describe rising figures.

. . . That may be a fair use of the word *trend*, but there is the other use with the implication of an ongoing process. So it might be better to use pure white hat thinking and to say: "For the last three years the figures show an increase in the number of women smoking." Then we can discuss what this means and what it may be due to.

In this sense white hat thinking becomes a discipline which encourages the thinker to separate quite clearly in his or her own mind what is fact and what is extrapolation or interpretation. It might be imagined that politicians would have considerable difficulty with white hat thinking.

CHAPTER 9

White Hat Thinking

WHOSE FACT IS IT?

Is it a fact or a likelihood?

Is it a fact or is it a belief?

Are there any facts?

We can now return to the statement I made at the beginning of the book about Rodin's *The Thinker* in that square in Buenos Aires. It is a fact that I was in Buenos Aires. It is a fact that a guide pointed out the Rodin statue. It is a fact that she seemed to claim it was an original. It seems to be a fact that it was in parliament square. The last two items are subject to the fallibility of memory. Even if my recollection is perfect, the guide may have been mistaken. That is why I prefaced my remark with "I believe." I chose to believe my memory and the guide.

Much of what passes for fact is simply a comment made in good faith or is a matter of personal belief at the moment. Life has to proceed. It is not possible to check out everything with the rigor demanded of a

40

scientific experiment. So in practice we establish a sort of two-tier system: *believed facts* and *checked facts*.

We are certainly allowed to put forward believed facts under white hat thinking, but we must make it absolutely clear that these are second-class facts.

. . . I think I am right in saying that the Russian merchant fleet carry a significant part of world trade.

. . . I once read that the reason Japanese executives have such large expense accounts is that they give all their salary to their wives.

. . . I believe I am right in saying that the new Boeing 757 is much quieter than the previous generation of aircraft.

The irritated reader might point out that these "weasel" phrases virtually allow someone to say anything and to get away with it.

. . . Someone once told me that he had heard from a friend that Churchill secretly admired Hitler.

The way is open to allegation, gossip and hearsay. This is quite true. Nevertheless, we do have to have a way of putting forward believed facts.

The important point is the *use* to which the facts are to be put. Before we act upon a fact or make it the basis for a decision, we do need to check it. So we assess which of the believed facts could be useful and then proceed to try and verify it. For example, if the believed quietness of the Boeing 757 is vital to the siting of an airport, then we certainly need to take that from the "believed" status to the "checked" status.

The key rule for white hat thinking is that something should not be put forward at a higher level than is actually the case. When the statement is properly framed as a belief, then the input is permissible. Keep in mind the two-tier system.

Let me repeat that we do definitely need the belief tier because the tentative, the hypothetical and the provocative are essential for thinking. They provide the frameworks which move ahead of the facts.

We come now to a rather difficult point. When does "belief" become "opinion?" I can "believe" that the Boeing 757 is quieter. I can also "believe" (opinion) that women smoke more because they are now under more stress.

Let me say at once that *your own opinion* is never permissible under white hat thinking. That would destroy the whole purpose of the white hat. You can, of course, report the actual opinion of someone else.

. . . It is Professor Schmidt's opinion that man-powered flight will never be possible.

Note very carefully that the belief level of fact simply means something which *you believe to be a fact* but have not yet checked out thoroughly. You might prefer to have the two tiers as:
1. checked fact
2. unchecked fact (belief).

In the end it is the attitude that matters. When wearing the white hat, the thinker puts forward neutral "ingredient" statements. These are laid on the table. There can be no question of using them to push a particular point of view. As soon as a statement seems to be used to further a point of view, it is suspect: the white hat role is being abused.

In time the white hat role becomes second nature. The thinker no longer tries to sneak in statements in order to win arguments. There develops the neutral objectivity of a scientific observer or an explorer who notes carefully the different fauna and flora without any notion of a further use for them. The mapmaker's task is to make a map.

The white hat thinker lays out the "specimens" on the table – like a schoolboy emptying his pockets of some coins, some chewing gum and a frog.

CHAPTER 10

White Hat Thinking

JAPANESE-STYLE INPUT

Discussion, argument and consensus.

If no one puts forward an idea, where do ideas come from?

Make the map first.

The Japanese never acquired the Western habit of argument. It may be that disagreement was too impolite or too risky in a feudal society. It may be that mutual respect and the saving of "face" are too important to allow the attack of argument. It may be that Japanese culture is not ego-based like Western culture: argument often has a strong ego base. The most likely explanation is that Japanese culture was not influenced by those Greek thinking idioms which were refined and developed by medieval monks as a means of proving heretics to be wrong. It seems odd to us that they do not argue. It seems odd to them that we cherish argument.

At a Western-style meeting the participants sit there with their points of view and in many cases the

44

conclusion they wish to see agreed upon. The meeting then consists of arguing through these different points of view to see which one survives the criticism and which one attracts the most adherents.

Modifications and improvements do take place in the initial ideas. But it tends to be a matter of "marble sculpture," that is to say starting with a broad block and then carving it down to the end product.

A Western-style consensus meeting is less fiercely argumentative because there are no outright winners or losers. The output is one that is arrived at by everyone and agreeable to everyone. This is more like "clay sculpture": there is a core around which pieces of clay are placed and moulded to give the final output.

Japanese meetings are not consensus meetings.

It is hard for Westerners to understand that Japanese participants sit down at a meeting without any pre-formed ideas in their heads. The purpose of the meeting is to *listen*. So why is there not a total and unproductive silence? Because each participant in turn puts on the white hat and then proceeds to give his piece of neutral information. Gradually the map gets more complete. The map gets richer and more detailed. When the map is finished the route becomes obvious to everyone. I am not suggesting that this process takes place at just one meeting. It may be stretched out over weeks and months with many meetings involved.

The point is that no one puts forward a ready-made idea. Information is offered in white hat fashion. This information slowly organizes itself into an idea. The participants watch this happen.

The Western notion is that ideas should be hammered into shape by argument.

The Japanese notion is that ideas emerge as seedlings and are then nurtured and allowed to grow into shape.

The above is a somewhat idealized version of the contrast between Western argument and Japanese information input. It is my intention here to make this contrast rather than to follow those who believe that everything Japanese is wonderful and should be emulated.

We cannot change cultures. So we need some *mechanism* that will allow us to over-ride our argument habits. The white hat role does precisely this. When used by everyone during a meeting, the white hat role can imply: "Let's all playact being Japanese in a Japanese meeting."

It is to make this sort of switch in a practical manner that we need artificial devices and idioms like the white thinking hat. Exhortation and explanation have little practical value.

(I do not want to get into an explanation of why the Japanese are not more inventive. Invention can require an ego-based culture with bloody-minded individuals able to persist with an idea that seems mad to all around. We can do it in a more practical manner with the deliberate provocations of lateral thinking, which I discuss elsewhere and also in the section on green hat thinking.)

CHAPTER 11

White Hat Thinking

FACTS, TRUTH AND PHILOSOPHERS

How true is a fact?

Of what value are the language games of philosophy?

Absolute truths and "by and large."

Truth and facts are not as closely related as most people seem to imagine. Truth is related to a word-game system known as philosophy. Facts are related to checkable experience. The practical-minded who are not much concerned with such matters can skip to the next chapter.

If every swan we happen to see is white, can we make the bold statement that "all swans are white?" We can and we do. For the moment that statement is a true summary of our experience. In this sense it is also a fact.

The first black swan that we see makes the statement untrue. So we have switched from true to untrue with remarkable abruptness. Yet if we are looking at facts,

one hundred white swan experiences are still set
against one black swan experience. So as a matter of
experienced fact we can say: "most swans are white";
"by and large swans are white"; "slightly more than
ninety-nine percent of swans are white."

This "by and large" stuff is immensely practical (by
and large children like ice cream; by and large women
use cosmetics) but of no use at all to logicians. The
"all" is essential in the statement "*all* swans are
white." This is because logic has to move from one
absolute truth to another: "If this is true . . . then this
follows . . ."

When we come across the first black swan, the
statement "all swans are white" becomes untrue.
Unless we choose to call the black swan something
else. Now it becomes a matter of words and definitions. If we choose to keep whiteness as an essential
part of the definition of a swan, then the black swan is
something else. If we drop whiteness as an essential
part of the definition, then we can include the black
swan and we base the definition of a swan on other
features. It is the design and manipulation of such
definitions that is the essence of philosophy.

White hat thinking is concerned with usable information. So the "by and large" and "on the whole" idioms
are perfectly acceptable. It is the purpose of statistics
to give these rather vague idioms some specificity. It is
not always possible to collect such statistics, so we
often have to use the two-tier system (belief, checked
fact).

. . . By and large corporations that base their spending
on extrapolated future sales run into trouble.

(It is possible to point to a few companies that have done this and been successful.)

... Sales will tend to rise if prices are lowered. (When house prices rise there may actually be increased sales for reasons of speculation, fear of inflation and fear of being left behind.)

... If you work hard, you will be successful in life. (A lot of hard-working people are not particularly successful.)

There is a spectrum of likelihood which might be expressed as follows:

always true
usually true
generally true
by and large
more often than not
about half the time
often
sometimes true
occasionally true
been known to happen
never true
cannot be true (contradictory).

How far along this spectrum is it permissible to go with the white hat role? As before, the answer to that question lies in the framing of the information. For example, it can be useful to know things that happen only very occasionally.

... Measles is usually harmless, but it can *sometimes*

be followed by secondary infections, such as ear infections.

. . . In *very rare cases* inoculation can be followed by encephalitis.

. . . When irritated this breed of dog *has been known* to snap at children.

Obviously there is a value in being aware of this sort of information. There is also a dilemma. In the second example given, people's perception of the danger of encephalitis following inoculation may be thousands of times greater than the actual statistical danger. So it can be important to give actual figures in order to avoid inadvertent misinformation.

Are anecdotes acceptable under white hat thinking?

. . . There was a man who fell out of an airplane without a parachute and survived.

. . . Ford is said to have designed the Edsel on the basis of market research and it was a total disaster.

These may indeed be statements of fact and as such the white hat thinker has the right to put them forward. They must be framed as "anecdotes" or "instances."

. . . Designs based on market research can often fail. Take for instance the Edsel car, the design of which is said to have been based on market research. It was a total failure.

The above statement is not legitimate white hat thinking – unless there is much more support for the claim that designs based on market research fail. Cats can fall off roofs but that is not normal behavior.

Exceptions stand out simply because they are exceptions. We notice black swans because they are usually in a tiny minority. We notice the man who survives a fall from an aircraft without a parachute because it is somewhat unusual. The Edsel is always referred to for the same reason.

The purpose of white hat thinking is to be practical. So we must be able to put forward all sorts of information. The key point is to frame it properly.

. . . All the experts predict that the interest rate will fall by the end of the year.

. . . I talked to four experts and each of them predicted that the interest rate will fall by the end of the year.

. . . I talked to Mr. Flint, Mr. Ziegler, Ms. Cagliatto and Mr. Suarez and all of them predicted that the interest rate will fall by the end of the year.

Here we see three levels of precision. Even the third level may not be good enough. I may want to know *when* you talked to these experts.

There is nothing absolute about white hat thinking. It is a direction in which we strive to get better.

CHAPTER 12

White Hat Thinking

WHO PUTS ON THE HAT?

Put on your own hat.

Ask someone to put on the hat.

Ask everyone to put on the white hat.

Choose to answer with the hat on.

Most situations are covered with the above statements. What it amounts to is that you can ask, be asked or choose.

. . . What went wrong with our sales campaign?

. . . To answer that I am going to put on my white hat. We reached thirty-four percent of retailers. Of these only sixty percent took the product. Of those who took the product forty percent took two items on a trial basis. Of the people we spoke to seventy percent said the price was too high. There are two competitive products on the market with lower prices.

. . . Now give me your red hat thinking.

. . . We have a poor product which is overpriced. We have a bad image in the market. The competition's advertising is better and there is more of it. We do not attract the best salespeople.

The "feel" aspects of the red hat thinking may be more important in this instance. But these "feel" aspects could not be put forward under the white hat except in reporting what potential customers had said.

. . . Let's start off by all putting on our white thinking hats and telling what we know about juvenile crime. What are the figures? Where are the reports? Who can give evidence?

. . . You have told me that you are going to order Prime computers. Could you give me your white hat thinking on that?

. . . I don't want your guesses on what would happen if we lowered our trans-Atlantic fare to $250. I want your white hat thinking.

It is clear that white hat thinking excludes such valuable things as hunch, intuition, judgement based on experience, feeling, impression and opinion. That is, of course, the purpose of having the white hat: to have a way of asking only for information.

. . . You have asked for my white hat thinking on why I am changing jobs. The salary is no better. The perks are no better. The distance from home is no different. The career prospects are the same. The type of job is identical. That is all I can say under the white hat.

CHAPTER 13

Summary of White Hat Thinking

Imagine a computer that gives the facts and figures for which it is asked. The computer is neutral and objective. It does not offer interpretations or opinions. When wearing the white thinking hat, the thinker should imitate the computer.

The person requesting the information should use focusing questions in order to obtain information or to fill in information gaps.

In practice there is a two-tier system of information. The first tier contains checked and proven facts – first-class facts. The second tier contains facts that are believed to be true but have not yet been fully checked – second-class facts.

There is a spectrum of likelihood ranging from "always true" to "never true." In between there are usable levels such as "by and large," "sometimes," and "occasionally." Information of this sort can be put out under the white hat, provided the appropriate "frame" is used to indicate the likelihood.

White hat thinking is a discipline and a direction. The thinker strives to be more neutral and more objective in the presentation of information. You can be asked to put on the white thinking hat or you can ask someone to put it on. You can also choose to put it on or to take it off.

The white (absence of color) indicates neutrality.

CHAPTER 14

The Red Hat

EMOTIONS AND FEELINGS

The opposite of neutral, objective information.

Hunches, intuitions, impressions.

No need to justify.

No need to give reasons or the basis.

Red hat thinking is all about emotions and feelings and the non-rational aspects of thinking. The red hat provides a formal and defined channel for bringing these things out into the open – as a legitimate part of the overall map.

If emotions and feelings are not permitted as inputs in the thinking process, they will lurk in the background and affect all the thinking in a hidden way. Emotions, feelings, hunches and intuitions are strong and real. The red hat acknowledges this.

Red hat thinking is almost the exact opposite of white hat thinking, which is neutral, objective and free of emotional flavor.

. . . Don't ask me why. I just don't like this deal. It stinks.

. . . I do not like him and I don't want to do business with him. That is all there is to it.

. . . I have a hunch that this bit of land behind the church is going to be worth a great deal in a few years time.

. . . That design is hideous. It will never catch on. It is a huge waste of money.

. . . I have a soft spot for Henry. I know he is a con man and he certainly conned us. But he did it with style. I like him.

. . . My gut feeling is that this deal is never going to work out. It is bound to end in expensive litigation.

. . . I sense that this is a no-win situation. We are damned if we do and damned if we don't. Let's get out of it.

. . . I don't think it is fair to withhold this information until after the deal has been signed.

Any thinker who wants to express feelings of this sort should reach for the red hat. This hat gives official permission for the expression of feelings that range from pure emotion to hunch. With red hat thinking there is *never* any need to justify or explain the feelings. With red hat thinking you can play the part of the emotional thinker who reacts and feels rather than proceeding from one rational step to the next.

CHAPTER 15

Red Hat Thinking

THE PLACE OF EMOTIONS IN THINKING

Do emotions muck up thinking or are they part of it?

At what point do emotions come in?

Can emotional people be good thinkers?

The traditional view is that emotions muck up thinking. The good thinker is supposed to be cool and detached and not influenced by emotion. The good thinker is supposed to be objective and to consider the facts in their own right and not for their relevance to his or her emotional needs. It is even claimed, from time to time, that women are much too emotional to make good thinkers. It is said that women lack the detachment that is needed for good decisions.

Yet any good decision must be emotional in the end. I place the emphasis on that phrase *in the end.* When we have used thinking to make the map, our choice of route is determined by values and emotions. I shall return to this point later.

Emotions give relevance to our thinking and fit that thinking to our needs and the context of the moment.

They are a necessary part of the operation of the brain, not an intrusion or some relic of the age of animal survival.

There are three points at which emotion can affect thinking.

There may be a strong background emotion such as fear, anger, hatred, suspicion, jealousy or love. This background limits and colors all perception. The purpose of red hat thinking is to make visible this background so that its subsequent influence can be observed. The whole of thinking may be dominated by such a background emotion. The background emotion may be attached to a person or a situation or it may be in place for other reasons.

In the second instance the emotion is triggered by the initial perception. You perceive yourself to have been insulted by someone and thereafter your whole thinking about that person is colored by this feeling. You perceive (perhaps falsely) that someone is saying something out of self-interest and thereafter you discount everything that person says. You perceive something to be an advertisement and thereafter withhold belief. We are very quick to make these snap judgements and to become locked in to the emotions they release. Red hat thinking gives us an opportunity to bring such feelings directly to the surface as soon as they arise.

. . . If I were to put on my red hat, I would say that your offer could be seen as furthering your own interests rather than that of the company.

. . . My red hat thinking tells me you want to oppose

the merger in order to preserve your job rather than to benefit the shareholders.

The third point at which emotions can come in is after a map of the situation has been put together. Such a map should also include the emotions turned up by red hat thinking. Emotions – including a great deal of self-interest – are then brought in to choose the route on the map. Every decision has a value base. We react emotionally to values. Our reaction to the value of freedom is emotional (especially if we have been deprived of freedom).

. . . Now that we have as clear a picture of the situation as we are likely to get, let's all put on our red thinking hats and give our emotional choice of action.

. . . Of the two choices – continue with the strike or negotiate – I prefer the first. I do not feel the time is right for negotiation. Neither side has been hurt enough to want to give up anything.

For those who see the value of expressing the emotions involved in thinking about a certain matter, the red hat idiom provides a useful means of legitimizing those emotions so that they can take their place on the final map.

But could red hat thinking ever draw out those emotions which must be kept hidden?

. . . I am opposing his appointment because I am jealous of him and his quick rise to power.

Would anyone ever really reveal such jealousy? Probably not. But the red hat idiom allows a way around this.

. . . I am going to put on my red hat and I am then going to say that I feel that opposition to the promotion of Anne may be based, in part, on jealousy.

Alternatively:

. . . I am going to take cover under my red hat and I am going to say that I am opposed to the promotion of Anne. It is just a feeling I have.

It should also be remembered that a thinker in the privacy of his or her own mind can choose to put on the red thinking hat. This allows the thinker to bring his or her emotions to the surface in a legitimate way.

. . . There could be an element of fear here. Fear of the hassle involved in changing jobs.

. . . Yes, I am very angry. And at the moment I just want to get my own back. I don't like being cheated.

. . . I have to admit that I am just not happy in this job.

Red hat thinking encourages the search: "Just what are the emotions involved here?"

CHAPTER 16

Red Hat Thinking

INTUITION AND HUNCHES

How valid are intuitions?

How valuable are intuitions?

How are intuitions to be used?

The word *intuition* is used in two ways. Both are correct. But in terms of brain function they are totally different. Intuition can be used in the sense of a sudden insight. This means that something which was perceived in one way is suddenly perceived in another. This may result in creativity, a scientific discovery or a mathematical leap forward.

. . . Shift attention from the winner to all the losers and you will quickly see that 131 singles entrants will require 130 matches to produce 130 losers.

The other use of the word *intuition* is the immediate apprehension or understanding of a situation. It is the result of a complex judgement based on experience – a judgement that probably cannot be itemized or even expressed in words. When you recognize a friend you do so immediately, as a complex judgement based on many factors.

. . . I have an intuition that this electric car is just not going to sell.

Such an intuition may be based on knowledge of the market, experience with similar products and an understanding of buying decisions at this price range.

It is this "complex" judgement type of intuition that I want to deal with here.

Intuition, hunch and feeling are close. A hunch is an hypothesis based on intuition. Feeling can range from a sort of aesthetic feeling (almost a matter of taste) to a defined judgement.

. . . I have the feeling that he will back down when it comes to the crunch.

. . . I have the strong feeling that this bus ticket and that bike are the vital clues in this murder hunt.

. . . I have the feeling that this is not the right theory. It is too complex and messy.

Successful scientists, successful entrepreneurs and successful generals all seem to have this "feel" for situations. With an entrepreneur we say that he or she "smells money." This suggests that the profits are not obvious enough to be seen by everyone but that the entrepreneur with a specially developed sense of money-smell can detect them.

There is nothing infallible about intuition. In gambling, intuition is notoriously misleading. If red has come up eight times in a row at roulette, intuition strongly suggests that black will come up next. Yet the odds remain exactly the same. The table has no memory.

So how do we treat intuition and feeling?

First of all, we give them legitimacy with red hat thinking. The red hat permits us to ask for feelings and also to express them as a proper part of thinking. Perhaps emotions and intuition should have separate hats, but that would only complicate matters. I believe it is possible to treat them together under the heading of "feelings" even though their natures are different.

We can try to analyze the reasons behind an intuitive judgement, but we are unlikely to be totally successful. If we cannot spell out the reasons, should we trust the judgement?

It would be difficult to make a major investment on the basis of a hunch. It is best to treat intuition as part of the map.

Intuition can be treated as one might treat an advisor. If the advisor has been reliable in the past, we are likely to pay more attention to the advice offered. If intuition has been right on many occasions, we may be more inclined to listen to it.

... All the reasons are against lowering the price, but my intuition tells me it is the only way to recover market share.

An experienced property man develops a sense of opportunity. His accumulated experience is expressed as an intuition which tells him which deals to make and which ones to leave alone. That intuition exercised in the property field may be very valuable because it is derived from experience. But that property man's intuition applied to the outcome of a presidential election may not be so valuable.

Intuition can also be handled on a "win some, lose some" basis. Intuition may not always be right, but if it has been right more often than wrong, then the overall result will be positive.

It would be dangerous to ascribe to intuition the infallibility of a mystic oracle. Yet intuition is a part of thinking. It is there. It is real. And it can contribute.

. . . Can you please red hat your intuition on this merger?

. . . My red hat feeling is that property prices are going to soar again quite soon.

. . . Give me a red hat on this new advertising campaign, will you?

. . . My red hat tells me this offer is not going to be accepted.

Where do intuition and opinion meet? We have seen that the white thinking hat does not permit the expression of opinion (though it may permit the reporting of the expressed opinion of others). This is because opinion is based on judgement, interpretation and intuition. The balance may be on the side of the judgement of known facts or on the side of feeling based on unknown factors. Opinions may be expressed under red, black or yellow hats. When the red hat is used, it is best to express an opinion as a feeling.

. . . My feeling is that boredom is responsible for much juvenile crime.

. . . My feeling is that the cinema box office wants a few spectaculars that are heavily promoted.

CHAPTER 17

Red Hat Thinking
MOMENT TO MOMENT

Reacting and getting upset.

This is what I feel about this meeting.

To show or to hide feelings.

Red hat feelings can be shown at any time in the course of a meeting, a discussion or a conversation. The feelings can be directed at the conduct of the meeting itself, not just the subject matter that is being discussed.

. . . I am going to reach for my red thinking hat and I am going to tell you all that I do not like the way this meeting is being conducted.

. . . I want to make a red hat statement. I feel we are being bullied into an agreement we do not want.

. . . Mr. Hooper, my red hat view is that you never listen to anyone else.

. . . I have said what I wanted to say and now I am going to take off the red hat.

Set against the natural flow of emotions that takes place during any meeting, the red hat convention might seem artificial and unnecessary. Do you really have to "put on" the red hat in order to be angry? Is it not possible to express emotions by means of looks and tone of voice?

It is exactly this *artificiality* that is the real value of the red hat. Normally emotions take some time to well up and even longer to die down. There is resentment and there is sulking. Offence is taken and offence is given. In a sense the red hat allows someone to switch in and out of the emotion mode in a matter of moments. You put on the red hat and you take it off. Views expressed under the red hat are less personal than views expressed without it, because it is recognized as being a formal idiom.

The very need to "put on" the red hat reduces the amount of bickering. No one can be bothered to put on the red hat every time he or she thinks there has been some slight. And once the red hat idiom is established, putting forward emotional views without its formality comes to seem crude.

Because the red hat provides a definite channel for feelings and emotion, these no longer need to intrude at every point. Anyone who feels the need to be emotional has a defined way of doing so.

It is no longer necessary to try and guess the feelings of others. There is a means for asking them directly.

. . . I want you to put on your red hat and to tell me what you think of my proposal.

. . . I suspect you don't like me. I want a red hat answer.

People in love like to hear their partners spell out the word even when they do not doubt the substance.

. . . Switching to a red hat level, I want to say that I am very pleased with the way this conference is going. Is that the general view?

. . . My feeling is that we all want to get this agreement settled and signed. Mr. Morrison can you red hat it for me from your point of view?

The red hat idiom should not be exaggerated or overused to the point of absurdity. It is totally unnecessary to formally adopt the idiom each time a feeling is expressed. The idiom is only used when a feeling is expressed or asked for in a defined and formal manner.

. . . If you make any more red hat statements, I am going to remove your red hat out of reach.

. . . Can we just have one overall red hat statement from you and then we'll leave it. What do you feel about this matter?

. . . I just want one opportunity to make a red hat statement. Then I am going to put away that hat and not use it again.

CHAPTER 18

Red Hat Thinking

THE USE OF EMOTIONS

Can thinking change emotions?

The emotional background.

Emotions as bargaining positions.

Emotions, values and choices.

Once emotions have been made visible by means of the red hat idiom, then an attempt may be made to explore and even change them. This itself is no longer part of the red hat idiom.

Thinking can change emotions. It is not the logical part of thinking that changes emotions but the perceptual part. If we see something differently than we did before, our emotions may alter with the altered perception.

. . . Don't look at it as a defeat. Look at it as a powerful way of finding out the weaknesses and strengths of his tennis game.

. . . Would this offer be acceptable if it were to come as an initiative from your side?

. . . Write it off as an essential learning experience rather than an error in judgement. Learning is always expensive. We won't have to go through it again.

It is not always possible to provide perceptions that can alter or evaporate emotions. But it is always worth a try.

Expressed emotions can provide the constant background to the thinking or discussing. There is a constant consciousness of this emotional background. Decisions and plans are seen to be made against this background. From time to time it is useful to imagine a different emotional background and to see how things would be different.

. . . We all know that these negotiations are taking place against a background of extreme suspicion. Let us try to imagine what our thinking would be if each side really trusted the other side.

. . . There is a feeling that what we decide here is not going to make much difference. Events have taken over. Let us imagine that this is not so and that we do have it in our power to control things.

. . . We do have to be conscious of the background of anger that is present. We cannot ignore it.

As I have indicated earlier, emotions and feelings are part of the coloring on the map. By means of the red hat convention we can get to know those "regions" which are highly colored from an emotional point of view. In designing solutions to disputes we can then keep clear of such areas.

. . . The proposed restriction on your work for competing companies is obviously a sensitive point. We'll keep clear of that for the moment.

. . . The union executive is never going to agree to anything that comes across as a wage cut. That has been expressed forcibly enough.

Emotions are often used to establish bargaining positions. I do not refer to sulks, threats, blackmail or appeals for pity. I refer to the emotional value that is ascribed to certain matters. The principle of variable value is at the base of negotiation. Something has one value for one party and a different value for the other party. These values can be expressed directly by means of red hat thinking.

. . . The ability to cross union demarcation lines is very important to our productivity.

. . . We must insist that the proper disciplinary procedures be followed. We are not saying that Jones is innocent but the procedures laid down must be followed.

It is generally agreed that the ultimate purpose of any thinking must be the satisfaction of the thinker. So in the end the purpose of thinking is to satisfy the expressed emotions.

Difficulty arises on three counts. Does the proposed course of action really work out to satisfy the expressed desires?

. . . I do not feel that lowering prices will actually increase sales.

The second source of difficulty is when the satisfaction of the desires of one party is at the expense of the other party.

. . . We can increase the overtime or take on more workers. The first would benefit those already working. The second would benefit some of those now out of work.

The third source of difficulty is the conflict between short-term satisfaction and long-term satisfaction. A basic tenet of Christianity puts this very clearly: What does it profit a man if he gains the whole world but loses his soul?

. . . We can raise the advertising rates and get more revenue immediately. But long-term we shall be driving advertisers to use other media.

. . . If we lower the price to attract customers from other airlines, we may get a temporary advantage. Then they will match our price and we may lose those customers again. But the lowered profitability will remain.

. . . I would really enjoy eating this plate of French fries, but it is not going to help my weight problem.

. . . I am going to put money into this play because I like Nerida, who is playing the leading part, and I want to see a lot more of her.

. . . I want to be seen as willing to back exciting new technology ventures, but long-term I know that steady growth is what my investors want.

Emotions are part of both the method of thinking and the matter to be thought about. It is no use hoping they will go away and leave the field to pure thinking.

CHAPTER 19

Red Hat Thinking
THE LANGUAGE OF EMOTIONS

Emotions do not have to be logical or consistent.

Emotions can be fine-tuned with language to match.

Resist the temptation to justify emotions.

The most difficult thing about wearing the red thinking hat is resisting the temptation to justify an expressed emotion. Such justification may be true or it may be false. In both cases red hat thinking makes it unnecessary.

. . . Never mind why you mistrust him. You mistrust him.

. . . You like the idea of an office in New York. There is no need to go into the details of why you like the idea. That could come later when we near a decision on the matter.

We are brought up to apologize for emotions and feelings because they are not the stuff of logical thinking. That is why we tend to treat them as an extension of logic. If we dislike someone, there must be a good reason for this. If we like a project, this must be based on logic. Red hat thinking frees us from such obligations.

Does this mean that we are free to have and to hold any prejudices we like? Is there not immense danger in this? On the contrary. There may be more danger in prejudices which are apparently founded in logic than in those which are acknowledged as emotions.

I am not opposed to the exploration of emotions and a probing for their foundation. But that is not part of the red hat idiom.

Emotions are fickle and often inconsistent. A question-naire asked Americans whether they were in favor of involvement in Central America. The majority favored involvement. Yet there was a majority against every single suggested method of involvement. It is possible to be in favor of involvement in the abstract but against it when the abstract is translated into concrete terms. Logically this may not make sense, but in the world of the emotions it does make sense.

The red hat convention is not a trumpet for the emotions, although some people may be tempted to use it in that way. It more closely resembles a mirror which reflects the emotions in all their complexity.

It is said that the Inuit (Eskimo) people have twenty words for snow. There are cultures that have as many words for the various nuances of love. English, and many other European languages, do not have a wide range of emotion-indicating words in common usage.

There is like/dislike, hate/love, pleased/not pleased, happy/unhappy. For example, we could use a word to indicate undecided-positive and another for undecided-negative. The word *suspicious* is rather too heavily negative.

Because red hat thinking allows us to be bold and open about our feelings, we can seek to fine-tune them to match the situation. Without the red hat we tend to be limited to the stronger words supplemented with tone and facial expression.

. . . I have a sense of your hesitancy on this deal. You do not want in, but you do not want to be left out either. You want to be on call in an antechamber. Ready to come in when it suits you.

. . . You don't dislike Morgan, but you feel uneasy about him. You would dearly like to have a good excuse to dislike him.

. . . We are simply out of tune on this matter.

. . . There is a sense of quiet deflation about this venture. Not a loss of enthusiasm but rather something resembling a very slow leak in an inflated rubber dinghy. You cannot see anything happening, but when you look again after a passage of time, it is clearly more flabby than before.

The red hat gives a thinker the liberty to be more of a poet with his or her feelings. The red hat gives feelings the right to be made visible.

CHAPTER 20

Summary of Red Hat Thinking

Wearing the red hat allows the thinker to say: "This is how I feel about the matter."

The red hat legitimizes emotions and feelings as an important part of thinking.

The red hat makes feelings visible so that they can become part of the thinking map and also part of the value system that chooses the route on the map.

The red hat provides a convenient method for a thinker to switch in and out of the feeling mode in a way that is not possible without such a device.

The red hat allows a thinker to explore the feelings of others by asking for a red hat view.

When a thinker is using the red hat, there should *never* be any attempt to justify the feelings or to provide a logical basis for them.

The red hat covers two broad types of feeling. Firstly, there are the ordinary emotions as we know them, ranging from the strong emotions such as fear and dislike to the more subtle ones such as suspicion. Secondly, there are the complex judgements that go into such types of feeling as hunch, intuition, sense, taste, aesthetic feeling and other not visibly justified types of feeling. Where an opinion has a large measure of this type of feeling, it can also fit under the red hat.

CHAPTER 21

The Black Hat

WHAT IS WRONG WITH IT

The logical-negative.

Why it will not work.

It does not fit our knowledge and experience.

Critical judgement.

The pessimistic view.

It has to be said that most thinkers – both trained and untrained – will feel most comfortable wearing the black hat. This is because of the Western emphasis on argument and criticism. Surprising as it may seem, there is a large body of opinion which believes that the main function of thinking is to wear the black hat. Unfortunately, this completely leaves out the generative, creative and constructive aspects of thinking.

Nevertheless, black hat thinking is a very important part of thinking.

Black hat thinking is always logical. Black hat thinking is negative but it is not emotional. The emotional-negative is the role of the red hat (which also covers the emotional-positive). Black hat thinking does look on the dark or "black" side of things, but this is always a *logical* blackness. With the red hat no reasons have to be given for a negative feeling. With the black hat logical and relevant reasons must always be given. In fact, one of the great values of the six thinking hats idiom is to separate in this definite manner the emotional-negative from the logical-negative.

. . . I don't think that lowering prices is going to work.

. . . That is red hat thinking. I want you to give me your black hat thinking. I want your logical reasons.

. . . In our past experiences – which I can put in front of you as sales figures – lowering prices has not resulted in sufficient sales to offset the reduction in profit margin. Our competitors also have a history of reducing their prices to match the competition.

Black hat reasons must stand on their own. They must be usable by anyone. They must be reasonable in cold print and not only when put forward in a persuasive manner by a strong character. Black hat thinking is based on the logic of match and mismatch.

Black hat thinking must be logical and truthful, but it does not have to be fair. Black hat thinking presents the logical-negative: why something will not work. The logical-positive – why it will work – is presented under the yellow hat. This is because the tendency of the mind to be negative is so strong that it has to have a specific hat of its own. A thinker must have an opportunity to be purely negative.

It is quite possible that there is a subtle difference in the brain chemistry when we are being negative and when we are being positive. If this is so, it would not make "practical" sense to have a hat for objective judgement that would cover both logical-positive and logical-negative because the brain chemistry would not flip back and forth all the time. The chemistry of the negative may be the chemistry of fear and the chemistry of the positive may be the chemistry of pleasure.

It is always claimed that the word *criticism* covers an honest appraisal of both positive and negative aspects. In practice, however, the verb *to criticize* implies the pointing out of what is wrong. This is exactly what is implied by black hat thinking.

Years of experience in the teaching of thinking have convinced me of the need to separate the logical-negative from the logical-positive. People who claim to be fair usually do no more than toss in a few minor points on the side opposite to their own view.

Although the black hat is the "criticizing hat," I do want to make it absolutely clear that it is *not* a matter of taking one side in an argument. There are no sides and there is no argument. The black hat focuses on the logical-negative. A thinker may switch from black hat to yellow hat and back again as he or she wishes.

. . . Wearing my black thinking hat I must point out the lack of an electricity supply in this cottage. Wearing my yellow hat I can point out that you do not have to pay electricity bills.

This specificity of the black hat relieves the thinker of the need to be fair and to see both sides of the situation. When he or she is wearing the black hat, negativity can be given full rein.

At first sight the black hat might be seen as enhancing the negativity that is already so characteristic of many thinkers. Just as the red hat legitimized emotions, so the black hat seems to legitimize this absolute sort of negativity. In practice the black hat has the opposite effect.

A person who is negative by nature will introduce that negativity at all times into his or her thinking. That negativity will always be there ready to pounce. This means that in our usual scrambled type of thinking – where we try to do everything at once – the tone will be mainly negative. By focusing directly on the negative, the black hat actually *limits* negativity. A thinker may be asked to remove the black hat. This signals a clear and definite switch away from the negative.

. . . Your black hat thinking has been superb. Why don't you put on a different hat for a moment or two?

. . . Throughout this meeting you have done nothing but black hat thinking. Is that the only hat you know how to wear?

. . . I want you to switch from the black hat to the yellow hat for the next five minutes. Tell me what you then see.

. . . We usually get our black hat thinking from Mary. When she is not wearing her black hat, she does not seem to have much to say.

. . . You are a one-hat-thinker. And it's the black hat.

A golfer who is excellent with his driver would not ignore his putter. Similarly a thinker who is good at black hat thinking does not like to feel that he or she is not also able to wear the other hats at will. In this way the hat idiom makes it clear that negativity is only one part of thinking.

It must by now have occurred to many readers that the black hat role is very similar to the traditional devil's advocate role.

. . . I do like this idea of an airship for passengers. But for a moment I am going to play the devil's advocate.

. . . We are being carried away by enthusiasm. Someone is going to have to play the devil's advocate and point out that the selling price is going to be much too high.

The black hat is indeed similar to the devil's advocate role and integrates that particular role into the whole series of roles symbolized by the six hats. In this way negativity is seen as just one of the thinking roles. There is, however, an important difference.

The devil's advocate was indeed an advocate appointed by the church courts to argue the case for the defendant accused of heresy or witchcraft. So here we are back to argument. As I pointed out earlier, black hat thinking has nothing to do with argument but only with focusing on the logical-negative.

Black hat thinking is used to fill in the black part of the thinking map. This black hat task is a task like any other. It needs to be done thoroughly. To hold back on black hat thinking because you fear that the negative

aspects will kill an idea is to destroy the whole purpose
of six hat thinking – which is that each of the six roles
should be played to the full.

CHAPTER 22

Black Hat Thinking

SUBSTANCE AND METHOD

Errors of thinking.

Why one thing does not follow another.

Rules of evidence.

Possible conclusions.

Just as in red hat thinking, black hat thinking can apply to the subject itself – I shall deal with this in a later section – and to the discussion or thinking itself: to the method of thinking.

. . . As far as I know that is an assumption.

. . . I do not see how that follows from what you have just said.

. . . The figures I know are different from the ones you gave.

. . . That is not the only possible explanation, but just one explanation.

. . . There need not be a logical connection between those points.

It would be silly and inconvenient if a thinker had formally to put on the black hat every time he or she wanted to make a remark of this sort. It is understood that such remarks are part of black hat thinking whether this is formally stated or not.

In practice it is better for a thinker to accumulate points of this sort instead of interjecting at every possible moment as in the usual argument mode. The thinker can then make a formal black hat statement, listing the various thinking errors that are claimed.

. . . I am going to put on my black hat for the moment because I want to point out what I perceive to be errors in this argument. The fall in the consumption of spirits may be due to health consciousness, but it may also be due to increased wine drinking or more severe drinking and driving laws. Also the increase in vodka sales may be due to increased advertising, and have nothing to do with the taste.

. . . As far as I can see you have all been giving a lot of opinions, assumptions and red hat feelings.

. . . That is not correct. Royalty payments are only exempt if the research and development work have actually been carried out in Ireland.

. . . I would like to black hat your thinking on this. The figures you gave are four years out of date. The sample is very small. And the figures are only from the south of the country.

I do not intend to set out here all the rules of logical deduction and inference. Many of these are abstract and not always relevant to practical matters – as distinct from closed systems.

We could simplify the basic rules as follows:

1. Is the basis sound and justified?

2. Does the derivation follow?

3. Does the derivation necessarily follow?

4. Are there other possible derivations?

By "derivation" I mean anything which is said to follow from anything else. Often a derivation is a conclusion.

. . . If we increase the prison sentences and penalties, that will reduce crime.

That may seem a logical enough statement. If we examine it in detail, we find that the derivation may indeed follow but not necessarily. If the risk of getting caught is known to be very low, then an increase in penalties may not be effective. If the courts do not impose the higher sentences, then the deterrent effect may be lost. Nevertheless, it could be said that an increase in deterrence is likely to have "some effect" in reducing crime. Here we come to an assessment of how large is "some effect." In terms of the extra cost of keeping people in prison it may be quite small. But we could go further. Might the increased penalties actually make crime worse? A criminal may be more inclined to kill his victim in order to reduce the chance of detection if the penalty is very severe. A longer stay in prison for a minor offence may turn the minor offender into a hardened criminal. Finally the higher cost of keeping people in prison might have less effect on reducing crime than spending that money on more police.

The interesting point to note in this example is that a great deal of *imagination* is needed to generate alternative consequences and possibilities.

As I wrote in *Practical Thinking, proof is often no more than lack of imagination.* This applies to science, to law and to most places other than the closed systems of mathematics and philosophical word games.

In practice one of the best ways of showing up a logical error is to put forward an alternative explanation or possibility.

. . . It is true that in many countries the number of divorces rises along with the number of washing machines, but this does not necessarily mean that washing machines cause divorce. Both trends may be due to increased affluence, the progress of society or to the increasing number of women in the labor force, etc.

. . . It is true that if we raise prices, sales are likely to fall. But if we can justify it as a premium product, we might get a different sort of buyer and the fall in sales will be offset by the increased revenue.

Here we get back to the "likelihood" aspect discussed under the white thinking hat. It is perfectly acceptable to point out a possible alternative, but there should never be a claim that every alternative is equally likely. The point to keep in mind is that black hat thinking is *never* argument.

How do we deal with error on the thinking map?

One person believes that increasing penalties would reduce crime. Another person feels that this is a possible but unproved assumption. Where possible, a reference to statistics or some actual experiment would be used to help decide the matter (white hat thinking). If the matter cannot be decided, the various alternative points of view are all put down on the map as possibilities. When the evidence is particularly weak, the possibility can be labeled as opinion. Any person using the map then has the choice of paying attention to that opinion or ignoring it.

. . . It is a reasonable assumption that holiday travel is going to increase because family incomes are increasing, there are less children and air travel will become relatively cheaper.

. . . It is possible that people will get bored with travel as the novelty wears off and they may opt for "second home" type vacations in their own countries.

Both possibilities would be noted. Both can coexist. Even when two possibilities are mutually exclusive, they should still be put down on the map until evidence or emotional preference makes a choice. Even a disputed fact can be put on the map – provided it is labeled as "disputed."

CHAPTER 23

Black Hat Thinking

PAST AND FUTURE SUBSTANCE

How does this fit my past experience patterns?

Is this so?

What are the risks?

We have looked at black hat thinking as regards the method of thinking. Now we come to the substance.

Are the facts right? Are the facts relevant? Facts are provided under white hat thinking but challenged under black hat thinking.

. . . The number of people unemployed may be under-estimated by the figures, because many people in a family may not bother to register.

. . . The 600 million air passages a year do not give any idea of how many people actually fly, because some people may make many trips. Also this figure includes short internal trips.

. . . The figures showing a fall in crime in the U.S. should be related to the population figures of each age group. It may be that the fall in crime is only due to the baby-boomers moving out of the major crime age of eighteen to twenty-three.

The challenging of figures and reports is one of the simpler and more obvious uses of black hat thinking. In such cases the purpose of black hat thinking is to point out that the facts are wrong (where this is the case) or to point out that the facts may possibly be inapplicable. If a major decision is to be based on the facts, then the possibility – even if slight – of their being inapplicable should lead to a search for improved facts or figures. The intention of the black hat thinker is not to create all possible doubt, as a defending lawyer does in court, but to point out weaknesses in an objective manner.

There is a great deal of experience that is not quantified in facts and figures. Black hat thinking can point out where a proposal or a statement does not fit such experience.

. . . In my experience, if you give people a bonus in the form of money, they quickly come to expect it as a normal part of their wages.

. . . In my experience people respond very well if they feel that extra effort is appreciated and if that appreciation is shown as some sort of tangible reward.

. . . If people expect to be rewarded, they will do very little unless a reward is offered.

The first two statements may fit the experience of

those sitting around the table discussing motivation. The third one may not.

It needs to be said that experience is very personal, and different people may indeed have different experiences. In different cultures, rewards may indeed have different effects.

It should also be said that different circumstances lead to different effects. It is possible that if rewards are too frequent, laziness may follow. For these various reasons, experience may appear incompatible or even contradictory.

... In times of inflation people tend to save more.

... That is not true. People save less.

In most countries people do tend to save more. But not in the United States. This may be because there is more financial advice and people are more sophisticated financially, or it may be because interest on borrowed money is tax deductible and in times of inflation interest rates may even be negative.

There are times when a black hat thinker may attempt to challenge something in absolute terms. This would apply to scientific facts, research findings, well-established data, etc.

... I think that is wrong. Most supermarkets make no more than two to three percent on turnover.

At other times the black hat thinker is justified in putting forward his or her own personal experience.

. . . I have found that working in a small organization is much more motivating. I disagree when you say that decentralized large organizations are like small organizations.

. . . I have to put on my black hat to tell all of you that what is proposed simply does not fit my experience of twenty years in the cosmetic business. You cannot have the same brand both as a premium product and a commodity product.

It is also the duty of black hat thinking to point out the risks, dangers, shortfalls and potential problems that might arise in the future.

. . . If we abandoned the first use of nuclear weapons, the Russians could over-run Europe with conventional weapons.

. . . I must point out that in these divorce proceedings your husband could claim that you were not a fit person to look after the children.

. . . If sterling continues to fall against the dollar, interest rates may have to be raised and that would bring about a fall in the stock market.

The only way we can look at the future is in terms of the past. This may mean a simple extrapolation.

. . . There is a firmly established trend for snacks and finger food. People are cutting down on large formal meals and taking up "grazing," which means that they nibble as they go.

. . . Many organizations have gone broke trying to sell

ice cream to the French. I do not see why this new attempt should succeed.

The future may also be interpreted as a coming together of different trends and patterns.

. . . As the working week gets shorter, there will be more leisure. But high unemployment means that many people with the leisure time will not have much money to spend on leisure. So we may need cheap forms of leisure.

. . . My black hat thinking tells me that Apple computers will get squeezed out of the market unless they become compatible with IBM machines. Buyers are going to want access to all the software written for IBM.

We can always be certain about the past – even though we cannot always be certain that a particular lesson from the past applies to a particular situation today. With the future we have to be speculative. Yellow hat thinking can be described as speculative-positive because it is optimistic and looks at all the good things that can arise from a proposed action or decision. One of the functions of black hat thinking is to provide the speculative-negative balance: "These things could go wrong."

. . . With regard to this proposed entry into the personal computer field, I must put on my black hat to give you my thinking. Can we make it at all? Can we put it on sale at the right price? What advantages will it have over the competitors? Why should anyone buy it?

Here we come to what may be called "negative question." The black hat thinker is virtually saying: "I have this negative view. It is up to you to convince me that I am wrong."

. . . Why do you think this consultant is going to be any better than the last one?

. . . What happens if the Japanese enter the civil aviation market?

. . . Where will we be if one of the major pharmaceutical companies starts making intra-ocular lenses?

Most negative questions can be put forward equally well in the form of: "I see a danger that . . ."

. . . I see a danger that the competition will match our lower prices.

. . . I see a danger that government subsidies will be terminated abruptly.

. . . I see a danger of overproduction of milk.

. . . I see a danger that rising wages will force up production costs and put us out of business.

. . . I see a danger that six hat thinking could become such a game in itself that no thinking is done about the subject matter.

Just as the devil's advocate is a traditional thinking role, so is that of Cassandra, the prophetess of doom.

This role fits exactly the speculative-negative aspect of black hat thinking.

How does one counter the negatives that are thrown up by black hat thinking? The first point to remember is that it is a mapmaking rather than an argument situation.

The first way is to note the negative and to acknowledge it.

. . . Yes, that is indeed a serious danger and should it happen we will be in trouble. We certainly need to keep it in mind.

The second way is to acknowledge the negative but to offer a parallel view that it is unlikely to be the case.

. . . There is that possibility but I think it is only a remote one. We have been testing this product for four years now and any failure should have shown up.

The third way is to acknowledge the danger and to put forward the proposed response.

. . . If the competitors do match our prices, then we shall launch our special low-price product, which has been designed to be sold at a very low price. If they try to match that, they will have no margin of profit left.

The fourth way is to deny the validity of the danger; in effect, to do some black hat thinking on the other person's black hat thinking.

. . . I don't see how that could happen because the cost of entry of any newcomer into this market is much too high. The major players are in place and we know about them.

The fifth way is to offer an alternative view and to place it alongside the black hat view.

. . . As oil prices become lower relative to other costs, people may start to go back to buying bigger cars, but once they are used to the convenience of smaller cars, I believe there will always be a market for them.

CHAPTER 24

Black Hat Thinking
NEGATIVE INDULGENCE

It is much easier to be negative.

It is more fun to be negative.

Yes . . . but.

Constructing a railway is a complex feat of engineering. A simple concrete slab placed across the line can derail an express. Placing that concrete slab is not a particularly skilled operation. Destruction is always much easier than construction. It is the same with negativity. That is why it is necessary when considering black hat thinking to consider also the attractions of negativity that so often lead to "negative indulgence."

Negative thinking is attractive because its achievement is immediate and complete. Proving someone wrong provides this immediate satisfaction. Offering a constructive idea does not provide any achievement until someone likes the idea or you can show that it works (which takes time).

Attacking an idea gives an instant feeling of superiority. Praising an idea seems to set the praiser somewhat below the originator.

Criticizing is very easy because all the critic has to do is to choose a frame of judgement and then show how the proposal does not fit that particular frame.

. . . What we need here is a simple, practical idea. What you have been proposing is much too elaborate and complex. It would never get off the ground.

If, however, the proposal had been simple and direct, then the critic would have chosen a different framework.

. . . This is too simplistic a view of the situation. That proposal is kindergarten stuff. My six-year-old son could have come up with something better. We have to take all the factors into account.

Note that both abrupt dismissals of the proposal are somewhat easier than the formulation of a new proposal. Note also that the criticism is not actually based on the substance of the proposal but on its general flavor as being "too complex" or "too simple." It is surprising how much criticism is, in practice, of this type. This sort of thinking should be placed under the red hat rather than the black hat.

. . . I do not like your proposal. It is as simple as that.

There is a great deal of red hat thinking which masquerades as black hat thinking.

. . . If that is all you have to say, then we must regard it as red hat thinking, not black hat thinking. You are entitled to your feelings.

It is much easier to make a suit that does not fit than to make one that does fit. This leads directly to the "yes . . . but" idiom. Here the negative thinker ignores the major part of the proposal, which is indeed valuable and workable, in order to focus on some minor part, which may be in doubt.

. . . The book is all right, but I wonder why she had to choose that absurd title. It says nothing about the book and has no relevance to it. It is the sort of title you might find on a trashy popular romance.

. . . The absurdity of the whole budget is seen in the imposition of VAT (sales tax) on take-out food. If the food is cold, there is no tax because it is just food. But if the food is heated, there is tax because now it is a "meal," not just food.

It is usually claimed that by pointing out the minor defects the critic is doing a useful service, because in effect he or she is saying: "Everything else is fine, so if you just put right that minor defect, then the whole thing will be perfect." No doubt this applies when a designer or writer is shaping the product, but when the product is ready then the idiom of the critic is: "I have to find something to criticize."

In the example of the tax on fast food, we see another idiom at work. Here the negative thinker sets out to give the impression that he or she is merely focusing on a sample of the whole. By showing that the sample is absurd, the implication is that the whole is equally absurd. This is equivalent to implying: "Any man who could do such a stupid thing is a stupid man. Therefore anything he does is stupid."

These are obvious and childish indulgences of the negative thinker. There are many others including adjectives ("feeble," "so-called," "childish," etc.) and the sneer ("well-meaning," etc.). There is also the traditional refuge of those who do not understand something new: "the Emperor's new clothes."

The dangers of negative thinking and the argument method are spelled out in much greater detail in my new book: *Conflicts: A Better Way to Resolve Them.*

Black hat thinking is meant to cover serious negative thinking and not the childish negative indulgence that I am outlining in this section.

The serious aspect of the "yes . . . but" idiom is that sometimes it is necessary to point out a danger that is not very likely to happen but must nevertheless be pointed out.

. . . I know you have tested these turbine blades for their performance in operating the jet engine, but do these new hyfil blades stand up to the lateral impact of a bird strike?

. . . It is not very likely but there is always the possibility that he may be a double agent. We have to keep that in mind.

. . . I suppose there is a possibility that books are now becoming expensive enough to be considered as legitimate presents.

Under white hat thinking I dealt with this matter of "likelihood." So long as something is appropriately framed (the likelihood given), then it is legitimate to put forward "yes . . . but" negative comments. These are offered as matters to be put right or matters to be kept in mind.

CHAPTER 25

Black Hat Thinking
NEGATIVE OR POSITIVE FIRST?

Should the yellow hat precede the black hat?

Fear and safety.

Curiosity and exploration.

Young children notice – and object to – the slightest deviation in a story that they know well. There is security in repetition.

It is reasonable to suppose that under conditions of fear an animal is designed to restrict its behavior to known patterns of fight or flight. Soldiers under fire are supposed to keep their discipline.

Is the negative aspect of mind a retreat to the certainty of what is known?

Which should a thinker put on first: the black hat of negative scrutiny or the yellow hat of positive exploration?

It can be argued that the black hat should always come first so that unworkable ideas can be quickly rejected without too much time being spent considering them. This negative screening is the way most people think and for many practical purposes it is swift and effective. When we are looking for competence rather than achievement, negative screening saves time.

It is, however, much easier to see the defects of any new proposal than to see its virtues. So if we use the black hat first on a new proposal, we are unlikely to take it any further. Once the set of the mind has been directed towards the negative, it becomes very difficult to see the positive. It may be that the brain chemistry has been set to "fear" and "security."

So when we are considering new ideas and changes, it makes a lot of sense to use the yellow hat *first* and to follow up with the black hat.

. . . In due course we shall get around to black hat thinking. But for the moment I want everyone to put on their yellow hats.

. . . That is black hat thinking. Keep it until later.

. . . I do not want black hat interjections no matter how valid. Note them down and give them to us later.

Once the idea and its claimed benefits have been spelled out, black hat thinking has something to work upon. I want to emphasize that it becomes everyone's business to use their yellow hat thinking on the proposal. It is not only the business of the person making the suggestion while everyone else sits silently, impatient to put on their black hats.

. . . You have not said anything yet. I want some yellow hat comments from you.

It could be claimed that if an idea passed through the negative "judgement" of the black hat and survived, then it would automatically be a good idea and yellow hat thinking would be superfluous. This makes the false assumption that all the merits of an idea are laid out on some sort of tray and all we have to do is to examine them. In fact, it requires a considerable effort of imagination and perceptual thinking to explore the merits of an idea. That is why deliberate yellow hat thinking is necessary – and that is also why it must come first.

Once the idea has been spelled out, black hat thinking can be applied in two ways. The first way is to examine the workability of the idea.

. . . Is this idea legal?

. . . Would this idea work?

. . . Are there any benefits in this idea?

. . . Is this worth doing?

I have chosen to include under the term *workable* the notion of benefit: if there are no benefits, the idea may be workable in the abstract but not in practice. Once it has been established that the idea is workable, black hat thinking can seek to *improve* the idea by pointing out the faults.

. . . If we did it that way, there would be a mountain of work at the end of each month.

. . . The system would be abused unless there was a personal code number for telephone shoppers to use.

Design improvement is a positive use of black hat thinking. Design improvement is certainly not limited to removing faults – imagining and achieving benefits is even more important. But the spotting and correction of faults and dangers is an essential part of design.

Occasionally it is possible to do more than just remove a problem. It may be possible to turn that problem into an opportunity or source of benefit. This would require a mixture of green hat thinking (creativity) and yellow hat thinking.

Black hat thinking is not concerned with problem solving – only with pointing out the problem.

CHAPTER 26

Summary of Black Hat Thinking

Black hat thinking is specifically concerned with negative assessment. The black hat thinker points out what is wrong, incorrect and in error. The black hat thinker points out how something does not fit experience or accepted knowledge. The black hat thinker points out why something will not work. The black hat thinker points out risks and dangers. The black hat thinker points out faults in a design.

Black hat thinking is *not* argument and should never be seen as such. It is an objective attempt to put the negative elements onto the map.

Black hat thinking may point out the errors in the thinking procedure and method itself.

Black hat thinking may judge an idea against the past to see how well it fits what is known.

Black hat thinking may project an idea into the future to see what might fail or go wrong.

Black hat thinking can ask negative questions.

108

Black hat thinking should not be used to cover negative indulgence or negative feelings which should make use of the red hat.

Positive assessment is left for the yellow hat. In the case of new ideas, the yellow hat should always be used before the black hat.

CHAPTER 27

The Yellow Hat

SPECULATIVE-POSITIVE

Positive thinking.

Yellow is for sunshine and brightness.

Optimism.

Focus on benefit.

Constructive thinking and making things happen.

Being positive is a choice. We can choose to look at things in a positive way. We can choose to focus on those aspects of a situation that are positive. We can search for benefits.

In attitude the yellow hat is the exact opposite of the black hat. The black hat is concerned with negative assessment, the yellow hat with positive assessment. Unfortunately, there are more natural reasons to be negative than there are to be positive. Negative thinking may protect us from mistakes, risk taking and danger. Positive thinking has to be a mixture of curiosity, pleasure, greed and the desire to "make things happen." It could be argued that man's progress depends on this desire to make things happen. In my book on success, *Tactics: The Art and Science of Success*, the one thing that characterized successful people was this overwhelming desire to make things happen.

I have termed the yellow hat "speculative-positive" because with any plan or action we are looking forward into the future. That is where the action or plan is going to be worked out. We can never be as certain about the future as we are about the past, so we have to speculate as to what might happen. We set out to do something because it is worth doing. It is our assessment of this "worth" or value that provides the "positive" aspect of speculative-positive.

Even when we look at something that has happened, we can choose to look at the positive aspects or extract a positive interpretation.

. . . The positive thing is that now we know how he is going to act. The uncertainty is over.

. . . Let's put on our yellow hats and look at the positive aspects. Kodak has decided to go into the instant camera market. So they will have to advertise their products. That will increase the public's awareness of the merits of instant photography. That should help our sales – especially if the public perceives that our product is better.

. . . Failing that examination was the best thing that could have happened to her. She would not have been happy as a teacher.

For a few people, being positive is a natural habit of mind. Most people will be positive when they are putting forward an idea of their own. Most people will be positive about an idea if they immediately see something in it for themselves. Self-interest is a strong basis for positive thinking. The yellow thinking hat does not have to await such motivations. The yellow thinking hat is a deliberate device which the thinker chooses to adopt. The positive aspect is not the result of seeing merit in the idea but precedes this. The yellow hat comes first. The thinker puts on the yellow hat and then follows its *requirements* to be positive and optimistic.

In the printing analogy that I used earlier, the yellow hat puts on the yellow color just as the red hat puts on the red color.

. . . Before you do anything else I want you to put on your yellow hat and to tell me what you think about this new approach.

. . . You have told me all the reasons why you do not like the idea and why it will probably fail. Now I want you to put your yellow thinking hat firmly in place. What do you see now?

. . . From a yellow hat point of view, can you see any merit in making this fitting out of plastic instead of metal? The cost would be about the same.

. . . I have this idea of selling potato chips in a twin pack. No one seems to like it. Will you yellow hat it for me?

. . . Right now I do not want a balanced view or an objective view. I want a definite yellow hat view.

. . . My black hat tells me that this new cheap lighter could hurt our sales. But my yellow hat tells me that the cheap lighter could kill the middle market and force some buyers up to the expensive market and so benefit us.

. . . It is hard to wear a yellow hat at the moment. But the newspaper strike could make people realize how much they missed their papers and how newspapers are much better than television for some things.

Although yellow hat thinking is positive, it requires just as much discipline as the white hat or the black hat. It is not just a matter of making a positive assessment of something that turns up. It is a deliberate search for the positive. Sometimes this search is futile.

. . . I am wearing my yellow thinking hat but I cannot find anything positive to say.

. . . I will put on my yellow hat but I do not expect to find anything positive.

It may be claimed that unless a positive aspect is obvious, it cannot really be worth much. It may be claimed that there is no point in cudgeling one's brain to find remote positive points that will have little practical value. This is to misunderstand perception. There may be very powerful positive points that are not at all obvious at first sight. That is how entrepreneurs work. They see the value that those around them have not yet spotted. Value and benefit are by no means always obvious.

CHAPTER 28

Yellow Hat Thinking
THE POSITIVE SPECTRUM

When is optimism foolishness?

From the hopeful to the logical.

What is realism?

There are people who will think well of a con man even after he has deceived them. They feel that he was sincere at the time and that he was let down by events or colleagues. They remember his persuasiveness and how they enjoyed being persuaded.

There are Pollyanna-type people who are optimistic to the point of foolishness. There are people who seriously *expect* to win major prizes in a lottery and seem to base their lives on this hope. There are industrialists who look at the huge aspirin market and feel that if they could only get a tiny part of it, it would be well worthwhile.

At what point does optimism become foolishness and foolish hope? Should yellow hat thinking have no

114

restraints? Should yellow hat thinking take no account of likelihood? Should that sort of thing be left to black hat thinking?

The positive spectrum ranges from the overoptimistic at one extreme to the logical-practical at the other. We have to be careful how we handle this spectrum. History is full of impractical visions and dreams which inspired the effort that eventually made those dreams a reality. If we restrict our yellow hat thinking to what is sound and well known, there is going to be little progress.

The key point is to look at the action that follows the optimism. If that action is to be no more than hope (like the hope of winning a lottery prize or the hope that some miracle will rescue the business), then such optimism may be misplaced. If the optimism is going to lead to some action in the chosen direction, it becomes more difficult. Overoptimism usually leads to failure, but not always. It is those who expect to succeed who do succeed.

. . . There is a remote chance that someone survived the crash-landing on the glacier. We must go and look.

. . . It is possible that this new party will split the opposition vote.

. . . If we invest heavily in promoting this film, we should have a success on our hands.

. . . There is a chance it might be chosen car of the year. We should be prepared to follow that up in our publicity. It may not happen but we have to be ready.

As with the other thinking hats, the purpose of the yellow hat is to color the notional thinking map. For this reason optimistic suggestions should be noted and put on the map. There is no need to assess them in detail before putting them on the map. Nevertheless, it is worth labeling such suggestions with a rough estimate of likelihood.

A simple likelihood classification can be drawn up:

proven
very likely, based on experience and what we know
good chance – through a combination of different
    things
even chance
no better than possible
remote or long shot.

This is somewhat similar to the one used for white hat thinking.

We may choose never to back a long shot, but that long shot needs to be on the map. If it is on the map, we have the choice of rejecting it or trying to improve the odds. If it is not put on the map, we have no choice at all.

. . . I know he is very busy and very expensive but get in touch with him and invite him to open the conference. He may just accept. At worst he can only say no.

. . . Every girl wants to be an actress and only a very few succeed, so the chances of success are not great. However, some people do make it, so try if you want to.

. . . You are not likely to find any hidden art treasure in a village antique shop. But then most hidden art treasures were in places no one expected to find them.

CHAPTER 29

Yellow Hat Thinking

REASONS AND LOGICAL SUPPORT

What is the positive view based upon?

Why do you think it will happen this way?

Background reasons for the optimism.

A positive assessment may be based on experience, available information, logical deduction, hints, trends, guesses and hopes. Does the yellow hat thinker have to spell out the reasons for his or her optimism?

If no reasons are given, the "good feeling" might just as well be placed under the red hat as a feeling, hunch or intuition. Yellow hat thinking should go much further.

Yellow hat thinking covers positive judgement. The yellow hat thinker should do his or her best to find as much support as possible for the proffered optimism. This effort should be conscientious and thorough. *But yellow hat thinking need not be restricted to those points that can be fully justified.* In other words, there should be a full effort to justify the optimism, but if that effort is not successful, the point can still be put forward as a speculation.

The emphasis of yellow hat thinking is on exploration and positive speculation. We set out to find the possible benefits. Then we seek to justify them. This justification is an attempt to strengthen the suggestion. If this logical support is not provided under the yellow hat, it is not going to be provided anywhere else.

. . . My yellow hat thinking suggests that omelettes would make good fast food items. If I look around for reasons to support that view, I might pick on diet consciousness and the preference for light foods. I might also say that as people tend not to have eggs for breakfast any longer, there is room to have eggs at other times.

. . . What about a range of action gloves? Not just gloves to keep you warm but gloves for working on the car, gloves for eating with, gloves for housework. People must do more for themselves today. They are also becoming more conscious of appearance and skin care.

CHAPTER 30

Yellow Hat Thinking
CONSTRUCTIVE THINKING

Making things happen.

Proposals and suggestions.

Imagine eight brilliant critical thinkers sitting around a table to consider means to improve the town's water supply. None of those brilliant minds can get started until someone puts forward a proposal. Now the full brilliance of that critical training can be unleashed. But where does the proposal come from? Who has been trained to put forward the proposal?

Critical thinking is a very important part of thinking, but it is by no means sufficient. What I so strongly object to is the notion that it is enough to train critical minds. This has been the tradition of Western thinking and it is inadequate.

Black hat thinking covers the aspect of critical think-ing. When dealing with the black thinking hat, I made it quite clear that a thinker wearing the black hat should play this role to the full: he or she should be as fiercely critical as possible. This is an important part of thinking and it should be done well.

It is to yellow hat thinking that the constructive and generative aspect is left. It is from yellow hat thinking that ideas, suggestions and proposals are to come. We shall see later that the green hat (creativity) also plays an important role in designing new ideas.

Constructive thinking fits under the yellow hat because all constructive thinking is positive in attitude. Proposals are made in order to make something *better*. It may be a matter of solving a problem. It may be a matter of making an improvement. It may be a matter of using an opportunity. In each case the proposal is designed to bring about some positive change.

One aspect of yellow hat thinking is concerned with reactive thinking. This is the positive assessment aspect, which is the counterpart of the black hat negative assessment. The yellow hat thinker picks out the positive aspects of an idea put before him or her just as the black hat thinker picks out the negative aspects. In this section I am dealing with a different aspect of yellow hat thinking – the constructive aspect.

. . . To improve the water supply we could build a dam on the Elkin River, thereby creating a reservoir.

. . . There is abundant water in the mountains fifty miles away. Would it be feasible to put in a pipeline?

. . . Normal flushing toilets use about eight gallons every time they are flushed. There are new designs that use only one gallon. That could save up to thirty gallons a day per person or nine million gallons a day.

. . . What about recycling the water? I have heard there are new membrane methods that make it economical. Also we would have less of a disposal problem. Shall I look into this?

Each of these is a concrete suggestion. Once a suggestion is on the table, then it can be developed further and eventually submitted to black hat assessment and yellow hat assessment.

. . . Put on your yellow hats and give me more concrete suggestions. The more we have the better.

. . . John, what suggestion do you have? How could we tackle this problem? Get your yellow hat on.

At this point someone would remark that proposals should come from the "water experts" and that it was not for amateurs to make such suggestions. It would be the role of the amateurs with their critical thinking to assess the proposals put forward by the experts. This is very much a political idiom. The technicians are there to provide the ideas and the politician is there to assess them. There may indeed be a role for this type of thinking in politics, but it does place the decision makers at the mercy of the experts. In other areas, such as business or personal thinking, the thinker is his or her own expert and must produce the ideas.

Where do the suggestions and the proposals come from? How does the yellow hat thinker come up with a solution?

There is no space in this book to go into the various methods of design and problem solving. I have touched on these subjects in other books of mine. The yellow hat proposals do not need to be special or very clever. They might include routine ways of dealing with such matters. They might include methods that are known to be used elsewhere. They might include putting together some known effects in order to construct a particular solution.

Once the yellow hat has directed the thinker's mind towards coming up with a proposal, the proposal itself may not be hard to find.

. . . Take off your black hat. Instead of assessing the proposals we have so far, put on your yellow hat and give us some more proposals.

. . . Keeping my yellow hat on, I suggest we let private enterprise sell water at competitive prices.

. . . No, we are not ready to switch into black hat thinking. I do not believe we have exhausted all possible suggestions. Yes, we do intend to bring in experts and consultants, but let us first establish some possible directions. So it's more yellow hat constructive thinking for the moment.

So yellow hat thinking is concerned with the generation of proposals and also with the positive assessment of the proposals. Between these two aspects there is a third. This third aspect is the developing or "building up" of a proposal. This is much more than the reactive assessment of a proposal. It is further *construction*. The proposal is modified and improved and strengthened.

Under this improvement aspect of yellow hat thinking comes the correction of faults that have been picked out by black hat thinking. As I made clear, black hat thinking can pick out the faults but has no responsibility for putting them right.

. . . If we hand over the water supply to private enterprise, there is a danger of the town being held to ransom by a monopoly supplier who establishes whatever price he likes.

. . . We could guard against that by putting a ceiling on the price. This would be related to today's pricing with an allowance for inflation.

I want to emphasize that no special cleverness is required by this constructive thinking aspect of the yellow hat. It is just the desire to put forward concrete proposals even if they are very ordinary.

CHAPTER 31

Yellow Hat Thinking

SPECULATION

Looking into the future.

The value of "if."

The best possible scenario.

Speculation has to do with conjecture and hope. Investors are by their nature speculators even if the word tends to be reserved for builders and currency operators. A speculative builder builds a house without already having a customer. Then he sets out to find a customer.

Any speculator must have a strong sense of potential benefit. There also has to be hope.

Yellow hat thinking is more than just judgement and proposals. It is an attitude that moves ahead of a situation with positive hope. Yellow hat thinking sets out to glimpse possible benefits and values. As soon as there is a glimpse of these, exploration takes place in that direction.

125

In practice there is a big difference between objective judgement and the intention to find positive value. It is this reaching out and reaching forward aspect of yellow hat thinking that I am indicating with the word *speculation*.

. . . There is a new type of fast food that is becoming popular. It is a sort of flattened chicken cooked in a Mexican style and offered as "pollo." Put on your yellow hat and tell me what you see in this.

. . . There are so many different types of insurance that people get confused. Could we have some sort of "overcoat" insurance that takes everything into account. Take that idea away and give it some yellow hat attention. Come back and tell me what you find.

This speculative aspect of yellow hat thinking is pure *opportunity* thinking. It goes beyond problem solving and improvement. People are forced to solve problems but no one is ever forced to look for opportunities. However, everyone is *free* to look for opportunities – if they so wish.

Speculative thinking must always start off with the best possible scenario. That is the way one can assess the maximum possible benefit from the idea. If the benefits are poor with the best possible scenario, then the idea is not worth pursuing.

. . . In the best possible scenario, the other store is forced out of business and we take over the whole business for the area. But I do not see that this would be especially profitable. As it is, the other store only just struggles along.

. . . In the best possible scenario, the interest rate rises rapidly and the value of our fixed rate transferable mortgage makes the house very saleable.

If the benefits seem attractive enough in the best possible scenario, it becomes a matter of seeing how likely that scenario is – and how likely are the benefits to flow as assumed.

In its speculative aspects, yellow hat thinking envisages the best possible scenario and the maximum benefits. Yellow hat thinking can then scale these down in a "likelihood" manner. Finally, black hat thinking can indicate the areas of doubt.

Opportunities can arise from the extrapolation into the future of the present scene. Opportunities also arise "if" some particular event takes place or some condition changes.

. . . Bond prices will rise "if" interest rates fall.

. . . "If" fuel prices fall, big cars will become more saleable.

It is part of the speculative function of yellow hat thinking to explore possible "if" changes.

It is never a matter of basing action or decisions on the basis of an "if" exploration – although defensive action may need to be taken as with the hedging of funds or the taking out of fire insurance. It is part of yellow hat exploration.

Part of the black hat function was also to explore "if" in the sense of risk and danger. The corresponding part of the yellow hat function is to explore the positive equivalent of risk, which we call opportunity.

. . . Under what conditions would this hotel chain become profitable?

. . . If satellite broadcasting gets established, what new opportunities is it going to offer to advertisers?

The speculative aspect of yellow hat thinking is also concerned with *vision*.

I mentioned the role of vision and dreams in yellow hat thinking in an earlier section. In a sense vision goes beyond speculation because vision can set a goal which there is little hope of reaching.

In any design there is some sort of vision that comes first. Just as a good salesman makes a sale by putting forth a marvellous vision which the client is invited to share, so the designer sells himself a positive vision of what he is trying to do. The vision comes first and then the form and detail follow. This vision includes both the benefits and the feasibility of the project: it can be done and it is worth doing.

It is very difficult to do anything at all without some sense of achievement and value.

. . . I have this vision of attractive low-cost housing, and I think I can also see how it could be done.

. . . I have this vision of a different type of economics which will handle wealth and productivity in a new way.

. . . I have this vision of thinking being taught as a fundamental subject in every school. It has already started in some countries.

The excitement and stimulation of a vision go far beyond objective judgement. A vision sets direction for thinking and for action. This is a further aspect of yellow hat thinking.

CHAPTER 32

Yellow Hat Thinking
RELATION TO CREATIVITY

Difference between constructive and creative.

Effectiveness and change.

New ideas and old ideas.

Yellow hat thinking is not directly concerned with creativity. The creative aspect of thinking is specifically covered by the green thinking hat, which we shall come to next.

It is quite true that the positive aspect of yellow hat thinking is required for creativity. It is true that the positive assessment and constructive aspect of yellow hat thinking is vital to creativity. Nevertheless, yellow hat thinking and green hat thinking are quite distinct.

A person may be an excellent yellow hat thinker and yet be totally uncreative. I see a great danger in confusing the two hats because then a person who is not creative would feel that yellow hat thinking is not for him or her.

Creativity is concerned with change, innovation, invention, new ideas and new alternatives. A person can be an excellent yellow hat thinker and never have a new idea. The effective application of old ideas is a proper exercise of yellow hat thinking. The ideas do not have to be new and there does not even have to be an intention to find new ideas. Yellow hat thinking is concerned with the positive attitude of getting the job done. Effectiveness rather than novelty is what yellow hat thinking is all about.

Some confusion occurs in the English language due to the very broad meaning of the word *creative*. There are two distinct aspects. The first aspect is that of "bringing something about." In this sense someone might create a mess. A carpenter creates a chair. An entrepreneur creates a business. The second aspect is that of "newness." Again this is confusing because there are two sorts of newness. The first aspect is of something which is new in the sense that it is different from what was there before; for example, a communications system that is "new" to your office even though it might be in use in thousands of others. The second aspect of "new" is an absolute newness. That is to say an invention or concept that has not occurred anywhere before.

In regard to artists, there is something of a dilemma. For example, a painter clearly brings into being something that was not there before. Since this painting is unlikely to be exactly the same as a previous painting, there is something "new." Yet there may be no new concept or new perception in that painting. The painter may have a strong style and then apply that style to one landscape after another. In a sense there is a production line within a particular style.

Yellow hat thinking is very much concerned with bringing things about. Yellow hat thinking may be concerned with taking an idea that is used elsewhere and putting it to work. Yellow hat thinking may be concerned with generating alternative approaches to a problem. Yellow hat thinking may even define opportunities. But yellow hat thinking is not concerned with changing concepts or perceptions. That is the business of green hat thinking.

Setting out to look at something in a positive way may itself create a new perception and that can occur with yellow hat thinking.

. . . That glass is not half empty but is half full of whisky.

Just as black hat thinking can pinpoint a fault and leave it to yellow hat thinking to correct the fault, so yellow hat thinking can define an opportunity and leave it to green hat thinking to come up with some novel way of exploiting that opportunity.

. . . More and more people need to park in cities. How can we get some value out of that?

. . . We could raise the room prices if we could attract more business travelers to this hotel. How could we do that? Let us have the usual ideas and then let us put on our green thinking hats in order to find some new ideas.

CHAPTER 33

Summary of Yellow Hat Thinking

Yellow hat thinking is positive and constructive. The yellow color symbolizes sunshine, brightness and optimism.

Yellow hat thinking is concerned with positive assessment just as black hat thinking is concerned with negative assessment.

Yellow hat thinking covers a positive spectrum ranging from the logical and practical at one end to dreams, visions and hopes at the other end.

Yellow hat thinking probes and explores for value and benefit. Yellow hat thinking then strives to find logical support for this value and benefit. Yellow hat thinking seeks to put forward soundly based optimism but is not restricted to this – provided other types of optimism are appropriately labeled.

Yellow hat thinking is constructive and generative. From yellow hat thinking come concrete proposals and suggestions. Yellow hat thinking is concerned with operacy and with making things happen. Effectiveness is the aim of yellow hat constructive thinking.

Yellow hat thinking can be speculative and opportunity seeking. Yellow hat thinking also permits visions and dreams.

Yellow hat thinking is not concerned with mere positive euphoria (red hat) nor directly with creating new ideas (green hat).

CHAPTER 34

The Green Hat

CREATIVE AND LATERAL THINKING

New ideas, new concepts and new perceptions.

The deliberate creation of new ideas.

Alternatives and more alternatives.

Change.

New approaches to problems.

Green is the color of fertility and growth and plants that grow from tiny seeds. That is why I chose green as the symbolic color for the thinking hat that is specifically concerned with creativity. The abundant creativity of nature is a useful background image.

The green thinking hat is specifically concerned with new ideas and new ways of looking at things. Green hat thinking is concerned with escaping from the old ideas in order to find better ones. Green hat thinking is concerned with change. Green hat thinking is a deliberate and focused effort in this direction.

. . . Let's have some new ideas on this. Put on your green thinking hats.

. . . We are bogged down. We keep going over the same old ideas. We desperately need a new approach. The time has come for some deliberate green hat thinking. Let's go.

. . . You have laid out the traditional approaches to this problem. We shall come back to them. But first let us have ten minutes of green hat thinking to see if we can come up with a fresh approach.

. . . This demands a green hat solution.

We need creativity because nothing else has worked.

We need creativity because we feel that things could be done in a simpler or better way.

The urge to do things in a better way should be the background to all our thinking. There are times, however, when we need to use creativity in a deliberate and focused manner. The green hat device allows us to switch into the creative role just as the red hat allows us to switch into the "feeling" role and the black hat into the negative role.

In fact, there may be more need for the green hat than for any other of the thinking hats. In the exercise of creative thinking, it may be necessary to put forward as provocations ideas that are deliberately illogical. We therefore need a way of making it clear to those around that we are deliberately playing the role of jester or clown as we seek to provoke new concepts. Even when they are not provocations, new ideas are delicate seedlings which need the green hat to protect them from the instant frost of black hat habits.

As I have mentioned at various points, the *signaling* value of the six thinking hats has several aspects to it. You can *request* that someone put on a particular hat and then attempt to think in that way. You can *indicate* that a certain type of thinking seems desirable. You can *signal* to others that you are trying to think in a particular manner – and therefore they should treat your contribution in the appropriate manner. One of the most important aspects is that you can also *signal to yourself.* This is particularly important with the green hat. You deliberately put on the green hat, and this means that you are setting aside time for deliberate creative thinking. This is quite different from simply waiting for ideas to come to you. You may have no new ideas at all while wearing the green hat, but the effort has been made. As you get better at deliberate creative thinking, you will find that the yield of ideas increases. In this way the green hat makes creative thinking a formal part of the thinking process instead of just a luxury.

For most people the idiom of creative thinking is difficult because it is contrary to the natural habits of recognition, judgement and criticism. The brain is designed as a "recognition machine." The brain is designed to set up patterns, to use them and to condemn anything that does not "fit" these patterns. Most thinkers like to be secure. They like to be right. Creativity involves provocation, exploration and risk taking. Creativity involves "thought experiments." You cannot tell in advance how the experiment is going to turn out. But you want to be able to carry out the experiment.

. . . Remember, I am wearing the green hat and I am

therefore allowed to say things like that. That is what the green hat is for.

. . . I thought we were supposed to be wearing our green hats. We are being much too negative. Isn't that black hat thinking?

. . . My green hat contribution is to suggest that we pay long-stay prisoners a decent pension on their discharge. That could help them get back into society, give them something to lose and prevent them from having to go back to crime. Treat it as a provocation if you like.

. . . Under the protection of the green hat, I want to suggest that we fire the sales force.

The green hat by itself cannot make people more creative. The green hat can, however, give thinkers the time and focus to be more creative. If you spend more time searching for alternatives, you are likely to find more. Very often creative people are only people who spend more time *trying* to be creative because they are more motivated by creativity. The green hat device allows a sort of artificial motivation. It is difficult to motivate someone to be creative, but you can easily request someone to put on his or her green hat and to give a green hat input.

Creativity is more than just being positive and optimistic. Positive and optimistic feelings fit under the red hat. Positive assessment fits under the yellow hat. Green hat thinking demands actual new ideas, new approaches and further alternatives.

With white hat thinking we do expect a definite input of neutral and objective information. With black hat thinking we do expect some specific criticisms. With yellow hat thinking we would like to get positive comments, but this may not always be possible. With red hat thinking we do expect to get a report on the feelings involved even if these are neutral. With green hat thinking, however, we cannot *demand* an input. We can demand an effort. We can demand that time be set aside for generating new ideas. Even so, the thinker may come up with nothing new. What matters is that time has been spent in the effort.

You cannot order yourself (or others) to have a new idea, but you can order yourself (or others) to spend time trying to have a new idea. The green hat provides a formal way of doing this.

CHAPTER 35

Green Hat Thinking
LATERAL THINKING

Lateral thinking and its relation to creativity.

Humor and lateral thinking.

Pattern switching in a self-organizing information system.

In writing about green hat thinking, I have used the word *creativity* because this is the word that is in general use. Many of the readers of this book will never have heard of me or of my concept of lateral thinking.

I also want to indicate that green hat thinking covers the broad range of creative endeavor and is not limited to lateral thinking as such.

I invented the term *lateral thinking* in 1967, and it is now officially part of the English language; the *Oxford English Dictionary* records my invention of the term.

The term *lateral thinking* needed to be invented for two reasons. The first reason is the very broad and

140

somewhat vague meaning of the word *creative*, as I indicated under yellow hat thinking. Creativity seems to cover everything from creating confusion to creating a symphony. Lateral thinking is very precisely concerned with changing concepts and perceptions; these are historically determined organizations (patterns) of experience.

The second reason is that lateral thinking is directly based on information behavior in active self-organizing information systems. Lateral thinking is *pattern switching in an asymmetric patterning system.* I know that sounds very technical, and there is no need to understand the technical basis of lateral thinking in order to use its techniques. The technical basis is, however, there for those who want to know on what it is based. Just as logical thinking is based on the behavior of symbolic language (a particular universe), so lateral thinking is based on the behavior of patterning systems (also a particular universe).

As a matter of fact, there is a very close relationship between the mechanisms of humor and the mechanisms of lateral thinking. Both depend on the asymmetric nature of the patterns of perception. This is the basis of the sudden jump or insight after which something becomes obvious.

The deliberate techniques of lateral thinking (various forms of provocation and "movement") are directly based on the behavior of patterning systems. The techniques are designed to help the thinker to cut *across* patterns instead of just following along them. The thinker cuts across to a new pattern, and when this is seen to make sense, we have the eureka effect.

Much of our thinking culture is directed towards the "processing" part of thinking. For this we have developed excellent systems including mathematics, statistics, data processing, language and logic. But all of these processing systems can only work on the words, symbols and relationships provided by perception. It is perception which reduces the complex world around us to these forms. It is in this area of perception that lateral thinking works to try and alter the established patterns.

Lateral thinking involves attitudes, idioms, steps and techniques. I have written about these in many places (*Lateral Thinking* and *Lateral Thinking for Management*). This book is not the place to go over them again.

I shall, however, deal with some fundamental points of lateral thinking in the following sections, because these points are also fundamental to the exercise of green hat thinking.

CHAPTER 36

Green Hat Thinking
MOVEMENT INSTEAD OF JUDGEMENT

Using an idea as a stepping stone.

Where does this take me?

The forward effect of an idea.

In normal thinking we use *judgement*. How does this idea compare to what I know? How does this idea compare to my established patterns of experience? We judge that it does fit or we point out why it does not fit. Critical thinking and black hat thinking are concerned directly with seeing how well a suggestion fits with what we already know.

We may call this the *backward effect* of an idea. We look backwards at our past experience to assess the idea. Just as a description has to fit what it is describing, so we expect ideas to fit our knowledge. How else could we tell if they are correct?

For most of our thinking, judgement (of both yellow and black hat types) is vital. We could not do anything

143

without it. With green hat thinking, however, we have to substitute a different idiom. We replace judgement with *movement*.

Movement is a key idiom of lateral thinking. It is another term that I coined. I want to make it absolutely clear that movement is *not* just an absence of judgement. Many early approaches to creative thinking talk about deferring, suspending or delaying judgement. I think this is much too weak, because it does not actually tell the thinker what to do – only what not to do.

Movement is an active idiom. We use an idea for its *movement value*. There are a number of deliberate ways of getting movement from an idea, including: extract the principle, focus on the difference, etc.

With movement we use an idea for its *forward effect*. We use an idea to see where it will get us. We use an idea to see what it will lead to. In effect we use an idea to move forward. Just as we use a stepping stone to move across a river from one bank to the other, so we use a provocation as a stepping stone to move across from one pattern to another.

As we shall see, provocation and movement go to-gether. Without the idiom of movement, we cannot use provocation. Unless we are able to use provoca-tion, we remain trapped within past patterns.

. . . I want you to use this idea for its movement value not its judgement value. Suppose everyone became a policeman.

It was just such a provocation which led to the concept of "neighbourhood watch," which I spelled out in the cover story of *New York Magazine* in April 1971. The concept is now in use in 20,000 communities in the United States. The idea is that citizens act as extra eyes and ears for the police – in terms of preventing and detecting crime in the neighborhood. There is said to be a significant fall in crime in areas where the idea is in use.

. . . Suppose we made hamburgers square. What movement could you get out of that idea?

. . . Suppose there were transferable insurance bonds which one person could sell directly to another. Green hat that idea.

This might lead to the idea that insurance was actually transferable. People would then be risk rated themselves. If you were an AAA type risk, you would get certain benefits from the universal insurance bond. If you were only an AA type, you would get lesser benefits.

Sometimes we take an idea and use it as a stepping stone and end up with an idea that is quite different. We merely extract some principle from the stepping stone and then apply that principle. At other times we stay with a "seedling" idea and nurture it until it grows into a stout plant. It may also be a matter of taking a vague idea and then shaping it into something concrete and practical. All these are aspects of movement. The key thing to remember is that we move *forward* with an idea or from an idea.

. . . Take the suggestion that everyone who wants to be

promoted should wear a yellow shirt or blouse. Put on your green hat and tell me where that idea takes you.

. . . It leads me to think of the self-image of the person who has chosen to wear a yellow shirt. He has to live up to that image.

. . . It leads me to think of some way for recognizing those people who have ambition but would not be noticed because of their talent. Maybe it would make more sense to train ambitious people and give them the skills.

. . . It leads me to think of the rules of the game. The yellow shirt would be a defined rule of the game of promotion and everyone would know it. How many employees know what they need to do to get promoted?

. . . It leads me to think of those people who do not want to be promoted. They can show this by not wearing the yellow shirt. They just want to stay in their jobs.

. . . It leads me to think of a way of bringing forward the leaders. A person would need to be pretty sure of his standing with those around before he risked putting on the yellow shirt.

From this sort of movement a number of useful ideas could emerge. None of these ideas need actually make use of a yellow shirt as such.

. . . Here is a suggestion for working on Saturdays and having a midweek break on Wednesday. Can you green hat it for me?

. . . As no one wants to work the weekend shifts, there is a suggestion that we employ a permanent Saturday/Sunday work force which would be quite separate. It seems an unworkable idea but green hat it.

In fact this last idea was tried out and worked very successfully. Using some green hat thinking on the idea made it seem attractive enough to be tried (in this specific case yellow hat thinking might have done the same).

Movement should go far beyond the positive assessment of an idea. Movement is a dynamic process not a judgement process.

What is interesting in this idea? What is different in this idea? What does this idea suggest? What does this idea lead to? Such questions are all part of the movement idiom.

The key point to remember is that in green hat thinking the movement idiom completely replaces the judgement idiom.

CHAPTER 37

Green Hat Thinking
THE NEED FOR PROVOCATION

Use of the word po.

The logic of the absurd.

Random provocation.

Scientific discoveries are always written up as if they had proceeded step by step in a logical fashion. Sometimes this is what indeed did happen. At other times the step-by-step logic is only a hindsight dressing up of what actually happened. An unplanned mistake or accident took place and this provided the provocation that set off the new idea. Antibiotics arose from the accidental contamination of a culture dish with the penicillium mould. It is said that Columbus dared to sail across the Atlantic only because he made a serious error in calculating the distance around the world from an ancient treatise.

Nature provides such provocations. A provocation can never be looked for because it has no place in current thinking. Its role is to jerk thinking out of current patterns.

The logic of provocation arises directly from the logic of asymmetric patterning systems (see *Po: Beyond Yes and No*).

We can sit around and wait for provocations, or we can set out to produce them deliberately. This is what happens in lateral thinking. The ability to use provocations is an essential part of lateral thinking.

In the preceding section we looked at the movement idiom. That is how we use provocations. We use them for their movement value. We can now look at how we set them up.

Many years ago I invented the word *po* as a symbolic indicator to indicate an idea was being put forward *as a provocation and for its movement value*. If you like, the letters stand for "provocative operation."

Po acts as a sort of white flag of truce. If a person approached the castle wall waving a white flag, it would not be playing the rules of the game to shoot that person. Similarly, if an idea is put forward under the protection of po, to shoot it down with black hat judgement would not be playing the game.

In a way – as I mentioned before – the word *po* acts in the same way as the green hat device. A person wearing the green hat is allowed to put forward "crazy" ideas. The green hat is much broader in scope than po but po is more specific. So it is best to use both.

. . . Po cars should have square wheels.

. . . Po planes should land upside down.

. . . Po shoppers should be paid to buy things.

. . . Po executives should promote themselves.

. . . Po a polluting factory should be downstream of itself.

This last provocation led to the idea of legislating that any factory built alongside a river must have its water input downstream of its own output. In this way the factory would be the first to sample its own pollution.

The word *po* may also be regarded as arising from such words as hy*po*thesis, sup*po*se, *po*ssible and even *po*etry. In all of these, an idea is put out for its forward effect – to provoke something.

By definition an absurd or illogical idea cannot exist within our ordinary experience. Therefore the idea lies outside any existing pattern. In this way a provocation forces us out of habitual patterns of perception. As we move forward from the provocation, three things might happen. We might be unable to make any movement at all. We might drift back to the usual patterns. We might switch to a new pattern.

Just as there are formal methods of getting movement from an idea, so there are formal ways of setting up provocations. These provide the deliberate techniques of lateral thinking.

For example, one simple way of getting a provocation uses *reversal*. You spell out the way something usually happens and then you reverse it or turn it back to front.

. . . Shoppers usually pay for the goods they buy. Let us reverse that. Po, the store pays the customers.

. . . This could lead to the trading stamp idea which, in effect, paid shoppers a tiny amount for each purchase.

. . . This could lead to the idea that the tills are rigged so that at every $1,000 of input they pay out a jackpot of some sort.

Provocations do not have to be absurd or illogical. It is possible to treat quite serious ideas as provocations. If someone brings you an idea which you do not like and which you can instantly dismiss with your black hat thinking, you could instead put on your green hat and choose to treat that idea *as a provocation*. It is always possible to make this sort of choice.

. . . I do not see how your idea of an "honor system" store could ever work because it could so easily be abused. But I am going to put on my green hat to treat it as a provocation. That leads to the idea of people adding up their own bills with random checks. Presumably mistakes would even out in each direction.

A very simple way of getting a provocation is to use a random word. You can think of a page number in a dictionary and then open the dictionary at that page. A second number you had thought of could give the position of the word on the page. For example you might think of page 92, eighth word down. Nouns are easier to use than verbs or other types of words. A list of nouns in common use is easier to use than a dictionary.

Suppose we wanted some new ideas to do with cigarettes. The random word turns out to be *frog*.

. . . So we have cigarette po frog. A frog suggests hopping, so we could have a cigarette that went out after a short while. This might be of benefit in preventing fires. It could also allow a smoker to have a short smoke and then to use that cigarette later. This in turn leads to a new brand to be called "shorts," which are indeed designed to be very short and only give a two- to three-minute smoke.

. . . I want some ideas to do with television sets. The random word is cheese, so television po cheese. Cheese has holes. Po the TV screen has holes. What could this mean? Perhaps there could be some "windows" which would show what was available on selected other channels.

With logic there should be a reason for saying something before it is said. With a provocation there may not be a reason for saying something until *after* it is said. The provocation brings about an effect, and it is the value of this effect which justifies the provocation.

To many people it may seem unthinkable that a random word could be of value in solving a problem. The definition of random means that the word has no special relationship. Yet in the logic of an asymmetric patterning system, it is easy to see why a random word works. It provides a different starting point. As we trace our way back from that new starting point, we increase the chance of arriving back along a track we would never have taken when thinking about the subject directly.

Just as movement is part of the basic idiom of green hat thinking, so too is provocation. When in France you talk French; when wearing the green hat you use provocation and movement as the grammar of creativity.

CHAPTER 38

Green Hat Thinking

ALTERNATIVES

Too easily satisfied.

Routes, options and choices.

Levels of alternative.

In school mathematics you work out a sum and get the answer. You move on to the next sum. There is no point in spending more time on the first sum because if you have the right answer you cannot get a better one.

Many people carry that idiom over into their thinking in later life. As soon as they have an answer to a problem, they stop thinking. They are satisfied with the first answer that comes along. Real life is, however, very different from school sums. There is usually more than one answer. Some answers are much better than others: they cost less, are more reliable or more easy to implement. There is no reason at all for supposing that the *first* answer has to be the best one. If time is very short and there are a great number of problems to be solved, there might be a reason for being satisfied with the first answer – but not otherwise. Would you like your doctor to settle for the first thing that came into his or her mind and then to stop thinking about your illness?

So we acknowledge the first answer and note that we can always go back to it. Then we set out to look for alternatives. We set out to look for other solutions. When we have a number of alternatives, then we can choose the best by seeing which one fits our needs and our resources.

We may have a perfectly adequate way of doing something, but that does not mean there cannot be a better way. So we set out to find an alternative way. This is the basis of any improvement that is not fault correction or problem solving.

So far in this section I have looked at instances where we already have a way of doing things. Our search for alternatives is really a search for a better way. There are also times when we do not yet have a way of proceeding.

In planning any journey we set out alternative routes. When we have completed the mental map of a situation, we look for alternative routes to our destination.

The notion of alternatives suggests that there is usually more than one way of doing things, more than one way of looking at things.

The acknowledgment that there might be alternatives and the search for these alternatives is a fundamental

part of creative thinking. Indeed, the different techniques of lateral thinking are directed to finding new
alternatives.

The willingness to look for alternatives (of perception,
of explanation, of action) is a key part of green hat
thinking.

. . . Our rival newspaper has just raised its price. Put on
your green hat and list all our alternatives.

. . . We have received a demand note saying that if we
do not pay a large amount of money, our products in
the stores will be poisoned. Let's go through the
obvious options open to us, then let's put on our green
thinking hats to find some further ones.

The search for alternatives implies a creative attitude:
the acceptance that there are different approaches. The
actual search for alternatives may not require any
special creativity until the obvious alternatives have
been spelled out. It may simply be a matter of focusing
attention on the subject and listing the known ways of
dealing with it. This is not sufficient. Just as we need
to make an effort to go beyond the first solution, so we
should make a creative effort to go beyond the obvious
set of alternatives. Strictly speaking we may only need
green hat thinking for this extra search. The first part
of the search could even come under white hat
thinking: "go through the approaches that are normally
used in such situations."

In practice it is more convenient to put the whole
search for alternatives under green hat thinking.

In business training a great deal of emphasis is put on decision making. Yet the quality of any decision depends very much on the alternatives that are available to the decision maker.

. . . We are going to have to decide on a location for this holiday camp. Put on your green hats and let me have all possible alternatives. Then we can narrow them down.

. . . How are we going to distribute these computers? What are the alternative strategies?

Many people believe that a logical scan will cover all possible alternatives. In a closed system this may be the case, but it is rarely so in real life situations.

. . . There are only three possible alternatives. We can leave the price the same. We can lower it. Or, we can raise it. There is nothing else we can do.

It is true that any possible action on the price must eventually fall into one of these three choices. Yet there are a huge number of possible variations. We can lower the price later (how much later?). We can lower the price on some of the product. We can change the product and produce a low price version. We can change our promotion of the product to justify a higher price (leaving the price the same or even raising it). We can lower the price for a while and then raise it again. We could leave the price alone and give special discounts. We could lower the price and then charge extra for options. Once we have considered such options (and there are many, many more), we could indeed classify them under one of the three choices.

But listing the three choices does not, itself, generate all these alternatives.

It is a very common fault of rigid thinkers to outline major alternative categories and to go no further.

. . . What I really want to do is to both raise and lower price at the same time. We shall create a low price commodity line and a high price premium line.

There are different levels of alternative. I have some free time. What shall I do with it? I could go on holiday. I could take a course. I could do a lot of gardening. I could catch up with some work.

If I decide to go on holiday, we move to the next level. What sort of holiday do I want? It could be a sun/sea holiday. It could be a cruise. It could be a sporting holiday. If I decide on a sun/sea holiday, we move to the next level: where do I go? It could be the Mediterranean. It could be the Caribbean. It could be the Pacific islands. Then there is the matter of choosing how to get there and where to stay.

Whenever we look for an alternative we do so within an accepted framework which sets the level. Usually we want to stay within that framework.

. . . I asked you for alternative designs for an umbrella handle and you have given me a design for a raincoat.

Occasionally we need to challenge the framework and to move upward to a higher level.

. . . You asked me for alternative ways of loading the

trucks. I am going to tell you that it would make more sense to send our product by train.

. . . You asked me to suggest media for the advertising campaign. I am going to tell you that the money would be better spent on public relations.

By all means challenge the framework from time to time and change levels. But also be prepared to generate alternatives within the specified level. Creativity gets a very bad name when creative people always make a point of solving a different problem from the one they have been given. The dilemma remains a real one: when to work within the given framework and when to break out of it.

We come now to what may be the most difficult point in all of creativity – the creative pause. The creative pause is not there unless we choose to put it there.

Something is going along very smoothly. We have looked for alternatives at the obvious points. We have spelled out different approaches to the problems. What more could we want from creativity?

I once spent ten minutes trying hard to turn off an alarm clock that was not ringing. I had not paused to consider that the sound might have been coming from my other alarm clock.

The creative pause arises when we say: "There is no obvious reason why I should pause at this point to consider alternatives. But I am going to."

In general we are so problem-oriented that when there are no problems we prefer to move along smoothly rather than to pause to create more thinking work for ourselves.

. . . I don't want you to think that we have a problem here because we don't. But I want you to put on your green hat and to have a little creative pause with regard to our normal habit of painting cars before we sell them.

. . . Have a green hat pause on this point: salesmen are paid commission on the sales they make.

. . . Consider the steering wheel of a car. It does its job well. Pause and green hat it.

CHAPTER 39

Green Hat Thinking
PERSONALITY AND SKILL

Is creativity a matter of skill, talent or personality?

Changing masks is easier than changing faces.

Pride in the exercise of a skill.

I am often asked whether creativity is a matter of skill, talent or personality. The correct answer is that it can be all three. But I do not give that answer. If we make no effort to develop the skill of creativity, it *can only* be a matter of talent and personality. People are much too ready to accept that creativity is a matter of talent or personality, and since they do not have this, they had better leave creativity to others. So I put the emphasis on the deliberate development of creative thinking skill (for example, through lateral thinking techniques). I then point out that some people will still be better at it, just as some people are better at tennis or skiing – but most people can reach a competence level.

I do not like the idea of creativity as a special gift. I prefer to think of it as a normal and necessary part of everyone's thinking. We are not all going to be geniuses, but then every tennis player does not hope to win at Wimbledon.

I am always being told about people who are natural black hat thinkers. They seem to take delight in destroying any idea or suggestion for change. I am asked if it might be possible to soften the personality of such people. I am asked if they could be made more tolerant of creativity even if they never want to use it themselves.

I do not think it is possible to change personality. I do believe that if a person is shown the "logic" of creativity, there can be a permanent effect on that person's attitude towards creativity. There are several instances in my experience where this has happened. The most practical approach is to use the green hat idiom.

. . . When you are wearing your black thinking hat you do a superb job. I do not want to diminish your critical effectiveness. But what about the green hat? See what you can do with that.

. . . Maybe you prefer to be a one-hat thinker. Maybe you are not an all-rounder. Maybe you can only sing one tune. Maybe you will have to remain the negative specialist. We shall bring you into the discussion only when we need black hat thinking.

No one likes to be considered one-sided. A thinker who is superb with the black hat would also like to be considered at least passable with the green hat.

The clear separation of green and black hats means that
the black hat expert does not feel that he has to
diminish his negativity in order to be creative. When
he is being negative he can be as fully negative as
before (contrast this with attempts to change
personality).

The tragedy mask and the comedy mask are separate.
The actor himself does not change. He plays each part
to the full depending on which mask he is wearing.
Indeed, he takes pride in being able to do both comedy
and tragedy. He takes pride in his skill as an actor.

In exactly the same way, a thinker needs to take pride
in his or her skill as a thinker. This means an ability to
wear each of the six thinking hats and to carry through
the appropriate thinking in each case. I did mention
this particular point earlier in the book. I am repeating
it again here because of this practical problem of
dealing with the negative personality.

. . . At this point we are doing some green hat thinking.
If you cannot do that, just keep quiet for the moment.

. . . You can at least try to use green hat thinking. You
will never develop any confidence in it if you do not
even try.

Creative thinking is usually in a weak position because
it does not seem to be a necessary part of thinking. The
formality of the green hat promotes it to being a
recognized part of thinking, alongside the other
aspects.

CHAPTER 40

Green Hat Thinking

WHAT HAPPENS TO THE IDEAS?

What happens next?

Shaping and tailoring ideas.

The concept manager.

One of the weakest aspects of creativity is the "harvesting" of ideas. I have sat in on many creative sessions where a lot of good ideas have emerged. Yet in the report-back stage most of those ideas have not been noticed or picked up by those at the session.

We tend to look only for the final clever solution. We ignore all else. Apart from this clever solution, there may be much else of value. There may be some new concept directions, even though there may be no specific ways of moving in those directions. There may be half-formed ideas which are not yet usable because they need a lot more work. New principles may have emerged even though they are not yet clothed in practical garments. There may have been a shift in "idea flavor" (the type of idea generated). There may have been a shift in the perceived solution area (where people are looking for solutions). There may be newly defined "idea sensitive areas" (areas where a new concept could make a big difference). All these matters should be noted.

It should be part of the creative process to shape and tailor an idea so that it gets closer to filling two sets of needs. The first need is that of the situation. An attempt is made to shape the idea into a usable idea. This is done by bringing in the constraints, which are then used as shapers.

. . . That is a great idea but in its present form it would be much too expensive. Can we shape it so that it is not so expensive?

. . . At the moment the building regulations would not permit us to do that. Can we shape the idea so that it does not contravene the regulations? Is that possible?

. . . That is the right product for a large company. But we are not a large company. Is there any way that we can use the idea?

Note that the constraints are brought in as shapers and not as a rejection screen.

The second set of needs that must be met are those of the people who are going to have to act upon the idea. Sadly, it is not a perfect world. It would be nice if everyone could see in an idea the brilliance and potential that is obvious to the originator of that idea. This is not often the case. So it is part of the creative process to shape the idea so that it better fits the need profile of those who are going to have to "buy" the idea.

. . . At the present moment there is only interest in ideas that save money. Is there any way this idea can be seen as saving money – now or later?

. . . To be acceptable an idea must not be too new. It must be seen to be similar to some old and tried idea that is known to work. What comparisons can we make?

. . . There is a great emphasis on being able to test out ideas in a pilot fashion. How could we test this idea?

. . . High tech is the new fashion. Would electronic technology improve this idea?

At times this process may seem to border on the dishonest. Yet there is nothing dishonest in designing a product for the buyer. So ideas need to be designed to fit the needs of the buyer (within the organization).

In some of my writings I have suggested the role of concept manager. This is someone who has the responsibility for stimulating, collecting and shepherding ideas. This is the person who would set up idea-generating sessions. This is the person who would put problems under the noses of those expected to solve them. This is the person who would look after ideas in the same way as a finance manager looks after finance.

If such a person exists, he or she collects the output of the green hat thinking. If not, the output stays with those who have generated it for their own use.

The next stage is the yellow hat stage. This includes the constructive development of the idea. It also includes the positive assessment and the search for supported benefits and values. Such matters have been discussed under yellow hat thinking.

Black hat thinking comes next. At any stage white hat thinking can be called upon to supply data required for evaluating whether the idea will work or will be valuable even if it does work.

The final stage is red hat thinking: do we like this idea enough to proceed further with it? It may seem strange to subject it to an emotional judgement at the end. It is to be hoped that this emotional judgement is based on the available results of black hat and yellow hat scrutiny. In the end if there is no enthusiasm for an idea, it is unlikely to succeed no matter how good it might be.

CHAPTER 41

Summary of Green Hat Thinking

The green hat is for creative thinking. The person who puts on the green hat is going to use the idioms of creative thinking. Those around are required to treat the output as a creative output. Ideally both thinker and listener should be wearing green hats.

The green color symbolizes fertility, growth and the value of seeds.

The search for alternatives is a fundamental aspect of green hat thinking. There is a need to go beyond the known and the obvious and the satisfactory.

With the creative pause the green hat thinker pauses at any point to consider whether there might be alternative ideas at that point. There need be no reason for this pause.

In green hat thinking the idiom of movement replaces that of judgement. The thinker seeks to move forward from an idea in order to reach a new idea.

Provocation is an important part of green hat thinking and is symbolized by the word *po*. A provocation is used to take us out of our usual patterns of thinking. There are many ways of setting up provocations including the random word method.

Lateral thinking is a set of attitudes, idioms and techniques (including movement, provocation and po) for cutting across patterns in a self-organizing asymmetric patterning system. It is used to generate new concepts and perceptions.

CHAPTER 42

The Blue Hat

CONTROL OF THINKING

Thinking about thinking.

Instructions for thinking.

The organization of thinking.

Control of the other hats.

Imagine a control panel. Operating that control panel is someone in blue overalls wearing a blue hat.

Wearing the blue hat we are no longer thinking about the subject; instead, we are thinking about the thinking needed to explore that subject. The color blue symbolizes overview control since the sky covers everything. Blue also suggests detachment and being cool and in control.

The conductor of an orchestra calls up first the violins and then the wind section. The conductor is in control. The conductor is wearing the blue hat. What the conductor does for the orchestra, the blue hat does for thinking.

Wearing the blue thinking hat we tell ourselves – or others – which of the other five hats to wear. Blue hat thinking tells us when to switch hats. If thinking is to be a formal procedure, then the blue hat is in control of the protocol.

Computers follow their programs which tell them what to do from one moment to the next. The blue hat is the programming hat for human thinking.

Wearing the blue hat we can lay out a plan for thinking with details of what should be happening in a defined sequence. We can also use the blue hat to give moment to moment instructions. The different ballet steps need a choreographer to arrange them in sequence. The blue hat is worn when we want to choreograph the steps of our thinking.

This notion of formally structured thinking is very different from the notion of thinking as a free-flowing discussion with no overall structure.

. . . My blue hat thinking definitely suggests that we ought to be looking for alternatives at this point.

. . . We do not have much time to consider this matter so we must use our time effectively. Would someone like to suggest a blue hat structure for our thinking?

. . . We have not got anywhere so far. Putting on my blue hat I would suggest we have some red hat thinking to clear the air. What do we actually feel about this proposal to decrease overtime?

Thinking often proceeds as drift and waffle and reaction to what turns up from moment to moment.

There is a background sense of purpose, but this is never spelled out either as an overall objective or as sub-objectives. Suggestions, judgement, criticism, information and plain emotion are all mixed together in a sort of thinking stew. It seems to be a matter of messing around until a thinker stumbles on some tried approach which seems to achieve what is desired. It is a haphazard exploration of experience strongly guided by negative criticism. The underlying assumption is that reasonably intelligent people provided with enough background information will, in the course of a discussion, list the action options and choose the most suitable.

There is also the assumption that the thinking will be moulded by past experience and present constraints in such a way that an outcome "evolves" and is purified by criticism. The analogy with evolution is a direct one for in Darwinian evolution there is survival of the fittest species and in thinking there is survival of the best-suited idea. For the harsh pressures of the environment, we substitute the harsh pressures of negativity.

In this type of thinking it follows that those taking part already have the proposals from among which the solution is going to be chosen. These proposals may have been arrived at through personal thinking or may have been provided by "experts."

In this book I am more concerned with the mapmaking type of thinking in which the terrain is first explored and noted. Then the possible routes are observed and finally a choice of route is made.

Those involved in a situation will claim that their thinking on the matter is taking place all the time and not just when they sit down for a formal discussion. Indeed, the purpose of such discussions is not so much to think as to exchange the results of the thinking that has already taken place beforehand. At this point we are getting close to the argument type of debate which is so typical of Western thinking.

I would be happy if I felt that a great deal of mapmaking thinking had gone on before the different views were designed. This is only rarely the case. The thinker quickly looks around for a view based on experience and prejudice and then seeks to have that view refined through argument. This is typified by the traditional method of writing essays in school. The pupil is encouraged to put his conclusion in the first line of the essay and then to use the essay to support that conclusion. Thinking is used for support not exploration. The same thing happens with politics and in the courtroom. Both sides start out with established positions.

The to and fro of argument provides the momentum for the thinking. That is why so many people find it easier to think in a group than on their own. Thinking on one's own has much more need of a blue hat structure.

If we are going to adopt the mapmaking type of thinking, we need to have structure. Attack and defence can no longer provide structure. Just as an explorer needs some plan of procedure, so the thinker needs some organizing structure.

A blue hat structure might provide a plan of what is to happen at every moment – rather like a computer program. More often blue hat thinking controls discussion-type thinking in much the same way as a coachman controls the horses by guiding them from moment to moment.

. . . White hat thinking at this stage.

. . . Now we need some proposals. That means yellow hat thinking. Concrete suggestions please.

. . . Just hold off your black hat thinking for a moment because I am not satisfied with the ideas we have. Let's have some green hat thinking at this point.

Most often it will be a matter of inserting the occasional thinking hat into an ongoing discussion of the traditional type.

. . . I want to get from each of you your red hat thinking on this. If you remember, when you are wearing the red thinking hat you are allowed to put forward your emotions and feelings without having to justify them in any way at all.

. . . You may not know it but you have been using black hat thinking – that is to say negative judgement. You have told us why it will not work. Now I want you to switch for a few moments to yellow hat thinking. This is where you make a positive assessment.

. . . I don't want your opinions or your suggestions. I want a few minutes of pure white hat thinking. The facts and the figures without interpretation.

. . . I think we need to pause and to do some blue hat thinking. Forget about the subject for the moment. How should we organize our thinking?

It should be said that blue hat thinking is not limited to organizing the use of the other hats. Blue hat thinking can also be used to organize other aspects of thinking such as the assessment of priorities or the listing of constraints. Blue hat thinking can also be used to orchestrate the use of the various CoRT thinking tools such as the PMI.

CHAPTER 43

Blue Hat Thinking

FOCUS

Asking the right questions.

Defining the problem.

Setting the thinking tasks.

The *focus* aspect is one of the key roles of blue hat thinking. The difference between a good thinker and a poor thinker often lies in the ability to focus. What should the thinking be about? It is not enough to be conscious of the broad purpose of the thinking.

. . . We want to focus on preparing a range of possible responses to price cutting by our competitors.

. . . Let's focus on what each of us wants from this holiday.

. . . Umbrellas and advertising. I want creative ideas on how ordinary umbrellas could be used for advertising.

. . . How can we get satisfied guests to encourage their friends to use our hotel? This is the specific focus.

. . . The broad focus is on new market segments to use

our fast food outlets. The tight focus is on getting old people to use our facilities at off-peak times.

A focus can be broad or it can be narrow. Within a broad focus there may be several tight foci. The important thing about a focus is that it should be *spelled out in a definite manner.* Blue hat thinking should be used specifically to bring about definition of the focus. Blue hat thinking should be used to monitor any drift from this focus. Time spent thinking about the thinking is not time wasted.

. . . I am putting on my blue hat to say that we have drifted very far from what we set out to think about. We do have a lot of interesting ideas but none of them are relevant to the starting focus. We need to get back on track. Any more blue hat comments?

. . . Put on your blue hats and say how you think we are doing. Are we getting anywhere?

Asking a question is the simplest way of focusing thinking. It is very often said that asking the right question may be the most important part of thinking. Unfortunately, it is much easier to ask the right question in hindsight – after the answer has been provided. Nevertheless, careful attention to the framing and focus of a question is an important aspect of blue hat thinking.

In the CoRT thinking lessons questions are divided into two types. There is a *fishing question,* which is exploratory (like putting bait on a hook but not knowing quite what might turn up). There is a *shooting question,* which is used to check out a point and which has a direct yes or no answer (like aiming at a bird and hitting or missing).

. . . The question is not so much what we do but when we do it. Timing is vital. What factors should we consider in this timing?

. . . The question is whether the tax advantages were really perceived by the client or whether they just provided our salesmen with a convenient selling point for insurance.

A problem is really only a special type of question: how do we achieve this? The definition of the problem is important otherwise the solution may be irrelevant or unnecessarily cumbersome. Is this the real problem? Why do we want to solve this problem? What is the underlying problem?

. . . The cold weather is not really the problem. People's perception of the cold weather is the problem. That we can change.

. . . The problem is not that we have no snow but that we have no skiing. So we take people in buses to where the snow is.

Instead of presuming to find the best problem definition, it is more practical to set out a range of alternative definitions. This is all part of blue hat thinking.

It is also the role of the blue hat thinker to set specific thinking tasks. This is even more important when an individual is thinking on his or her own.

. . . Set out the objective of this meeting. What sort of outcome would we regard as successful?

. . . Start by listing the areas of agreement between the two parties.

. . . The thinking task is to figure out how we might decide this point here and now.

. . . List four "idea sensitive areas" to do with school education.

. . . Black hat our current advertising campaign.

A thinking task may be bite-sized or it may be broad. A thinking task may require a specific achievement or it may ask for input within an area.

. . . I just want some exploratory ideas on this business of shopping via the TV set.

. . . How can we find out whether their strategy has been successful?

. . . Why are we having difficulty in deciding between these alternatives?

When a thinking task cannot be carried out then a note of that failure needs to be made.

. . . We have not come up with an explanation of this increase in candy eating. We shall have to come back to it later and see if we can produce some testable hypotheses.

. . . We have not come up with any ideas for increasing

the consumption of lamb. Perhaps we had better break it down into sub-problems.

The blue hat thinker holds up the target and says, "This is it. Shoot in this direction."

CHAPTER 44

Blue Hat Thinking

PROGRAM DESIGN

Step by step.

Software for thinking.

Choreography.

Computers have their software which tells them what to do at every instant. Without software a computer cannot work. One of the functions of blue hat thinking is to design software for thinking about a particular matter. It is possible to have fixed structures which can be applied to any situation. In one of the CoRT sections I put forward just such a structure called PISCO (Purpose, Input, Solutions, Choice, Operation). What I want to look at in this section is customized software which is designed for each situation.

. . . We will start with some blue hat thinking to design the program we want to follow.

. . . This is an unusual situation. Where do we start? What should we be thinking about?

At the end of the last section I mentioned that most of the time six hat thinking will consist of occasional interventions in the course of normal discussion/ argument type thinking. There will be occasional requests for a specific type of thinking symbolized by a thinking hat. Here I want to consider the formal program possibility which does lay down a sequence of steps.

There is free dance in which the dancers improvise from moment to moment in order to express the overall theme. Then there is formal ballet in which each step is precisely determined by the choreography. It is this choreography aspect of blue hat thinking that I am concerned with here. But I do not want the reader to think that this is the way six hat thinking should be used all the time.

I also want to make clear – as I have done before – that blue hat programs can include many more aspects of thinking than just the six hats.

. . . We should start by analyzing all the factors that we must take into account in designing this line of children's clothes.

. . . We should start by mapping out the areas of agreement, the areas of disagreement and the areas of irrelevance in this dispute.

The last mentioned procedure is known as the A.D.I. and is one of the CoRT tools.

The program will vary from situation to situation. The program for solving a problem will differ from the program used to design a boat. A negotiations program will not be the same as a decision program. Even within the area of decision making, the program used for one decision may differ from that used for another. The blue hat thinker customizes the program to fit the situation, just as a carpenter plans how he is going to make a chair or a cabinet.

Should the subject be one about which the thinkers have strong feelings, then it would make sense to put red hat thinking first on the program. This would bring the feelings to the surface and make them visible. Without this red hat thinking each person might seek to express his or her emotions indirectly through other means, such as excessive black hat thinking. Once the emotions are made visible, then a thinker is more free of them. There may even be more pressure on that thinker to be objective.

The next step might be white hat thinking so that all the relevant information can be put on the table. It is usually necessary to go back to white hat thinking from time to time – as a sort of sub-routine – in order to check out different points.

Yellow hat thinking is then used to put forward existing proposals and suggestions. There can be an interplay between blue hat thinking and yellow hat thinking as the blue hat thinking asks questions and pinpoints problem areas. White hat thinking can also put forward "state of the art" approaches to the problem.

. . . In the past what we have done in these situations is as follows.

. . . The traditional approaches are known to you all. Nevertheless, I shall repeat them.

Blue hat thinking might define focus areas that need new concepts. Green hat thinking would then try to generate some new concepts. Alternatively, there could be a formal green hat period in which each individual thinker carried out his or her own creative pause.

. . . I would like to see if there might be any simpler ways of adjusting premium payments to an individual's cash flow.

. . . There has to be a better way of selling books. I want to green hat that.

At this point a spell of blue hat thinking would organize the available proposals so that there was a formal list. The proposals might then be put into different categories: those requiring individual appraisal, those requiring further amplification, those which just need to be noted.

A mixture of white hat, yellow hat and green hat thinking might now take place in order to develop and take further each of the proposals. This is the constructive thinking phase.

Pure yellow hat thinking is now used to give a positive assessment to each of the alternatives that are regarded as serious possibilities.

Black hat thinking is now used in a screening sense. The purpose of black hat thinking is to point out which alternatives are impossible or unusable. Black hat thinking can also challenge the value of alternatives that are usable.

Yellow hat and green hat thinking is now used to overcome the objectives made by black hat thinking: faults are to be corrected; weaknesses are to be removed; problems are to be solved.

There is a further black hat scrutiny to point out risks, dangers and shortfalls.

Next might follow a blue hat spell which puts together an overview of what has been achieved and also organizes the "choice of route" strategy.

Red hat thinking now follows to allow the thinkers to express their feelings on the available choices.

The choice procedure now follows as a mixture of yellow and black hat thinking – looking for the alternative that best fits the needs.

Finally a blue hat session sets out the strategy for thinking about implementation.

All this may seem a rather complex sequence, but in practice each idiom flows naturally into the next one – like changing gears when driving.

Where there is to be a fixed program, it is essential that it be made visible to each person taking part in the thinking. If a thinker knows that a black hat session will be coming up shortly, he or she will feel less compelled to put in black hat interjections for fear that otherwise a point will slip by.

It should be remembered that most thinking is actually a mixture of black and white hats – with unexpressed red hat emotions in the background.

. . . This is what we need to do on this sort of occasion.

. . . This is why what you suggest will not work.

The blue hat program can be predetermined by someone who is leading the thinking session or it can be designed by blue hat thinking on the part of all present at the session.

CHAPTER 45

Blue Hat Thinking
SUMMARIES AND CONCLUSIONS

Observation and overview.

Comment.

Summaries, conclusions, harvesting and reports.

The blue hat thinker is looking at the thinking that is taking place. He is the choreographer who designs the steps, but he is also the critic who watches what is happening. The blue hat thinker is not driving the car along the road, but he is watching the driver. He is also noting the route that is being taken.

The blue hat thinker can make comments on what he or she observes.

. . . We are spending too much time arguing about this point. Let us just note it down as a point on which there are conflicting views.

. . . We seem to be much concerned with the cost of this operation, but we have not yet determined if it would provide any benefit. Surely that should come first.

. . . David, you keep pushing this same idea all the time. We do have a note of it as a strong possibility and we will examine it later. I think we should try for some further alternatives. This is meant to be an exploration not an argument.

From time to time the blue hat thinker gives an overview of what has been happening and what has been achieved. He or she is the person who stands by the flip chart and sets out to list the generated alternatives.

. . . Let's summarize what we have achieved so far.

. . . I am going to go through the major points that we have discussed. If someone disagrees with my summary, let me know.

It is the task of the blue hat thinker to pull into shape what may seem to have been a chaotic discussion.

Although I refer to the blue hat thinker as a single person, it is always possible for these blue hat tasks to be carried out by all members of the group. Indeed, one blue hat thinker can ask everyone else to put on the blue hat and carry out the task.

. . . I suggest we pause here. I suggest we all put on our blue hats and spend the next few minutes individually summarizing what we feel has been achieved so far.

. . . Let's go around the table. Put on your blue hats and tell me where we have got to.

Just as it is the role of the blue hat thinker to summarize what has been achieved from time to time, so it is also a blue hat function to pull together the final conclusions.

. . . Wearing my blue hat it seems to me that our conclusions are as follows.

. . . Are we all agreed that these are the conclusions that we reached?

It is the business of blue hat thinking to make the final summary and prepare the report. This does not mean that it is the role of one individual (though it may be). It means that each thinker switches into his blue hat role to comment accurately and objectively on the thinking that has taken place.

One of the blue hat functions is to be a photographer who observes and records the thinking that is taking place and has taken place.

CHAPTER 46

Blue Hat Thinking

CONTROL AND MONITORING

The chairperson.

Discipline and focus.

Who is in charge?

Normally the chairperson at any meeting has an automatic blue hat function. He or she keeps order and makes sure that the agenda is observed.

It is possible to assign a specific blue hat role to someone other than the chairperson. This blue hat thinker will then have the task of monitoring the thinking within the framework set by the chairperson. It may well be that the chairperson is not himself or herself particularly skilled in monitoring thinking.

I also want to emphasize that anyone at a meeting can exercise a blue hat function.

. . . I am reaching for my blue thinking hat to say that Ms. Brown's comments are inappropriate at this point.

. . . I am going to put on my blue hat in order to say

190

that I think we are straying away from the central issue.

. . . My blue hat thinking tells me that we should define this point as a key problem, then we should attempt to tackle this problem – now or later.

Blue hat thinking makes sure that the rules of the game are observed. This discipline aspect may be the role of the chairperson or the appointed blue hat thinker, but it is also open to anyone to comment.

. . . This is red hat thinking. We want your feelings, not why you hold them.

. . . I am sorry, that is clearly black hàt thinking and out of order at this point.

. . . That is not the way to treat an idea under green hat thinking. You are supposed to use movement not judgement.

. . . Is that really supposed to be white hat information? It seems more like red hat feeling.

. . . The blue hat role is to summarize the thinking that has taken place, not to argue in favor of one alternative.

In practice there is quite a lot of overlap between the different hats and there is no need to be pedantic about it. There may be a lot of overlap between yellow hat and green hat thinking. There may be a lot of overlap between white hat and red hat thinking due to mixtures of facts and opinions.

It is also impractical to keep switching hats with every remark one makes.

What is important is that if a defined thinking mode has been set the thinkers *should be making a conscious effort* to think in that manner. If it is to be yellow hat thinking, then it must be yellow hat thinking.

When no specific hat has been requested, it is unnecessary to suppose that every single comment must fall under one hat or another. It is also perfectly in order for someone to interject a procedural comment without formally indicating that he is using the blue hat.

On the other hand, it is very important formally to identify the hats from time to time. It is not enough to suppose that the type of hat will follow from the remark. It is precisely the discipline of trying to follow a thinking mode that is important. Otherwise we are back to the waffle and argument mode.

One of the major tasks of blue hat control will be to break up arguments.

. . . I think the increase in turkey meat sales is due to health consciousness.

. . . I think it is simply due to the cheaper price.

At this point a blue hat thinker might ask if there is any white hat information that might settle the point.

. . . As we cannot settle this point, we should note down that there are two offered explanations for this trend. We do not have to decide which is the right one.

So both points are put on the thinking map. In this particular case both points of view may be correct. At other times the two views may be mutually incompatible. Nevertheless, both views can be noted down. Further discussion can take place later.

. . . We can now come back to that point we could not decide upon earlier. Would this be seen as predatory pricing? Let us now focus directly upon that point.

. . . Mr. Jones thinks that a guarantee on holiday prices will make a big difference to sales. Ms. Adams thinks that it will not and that it could prove very expensive. Let's spend some time examining this point. What does white hat thinking have to offer? If we had had such a guarantee in past years, what would it have cost us?

A powerful way of treating opposing ideas is to suppose that each one is correct *under certain circumstances*.

. . . Under what circumstances would Mr. Jones be right? Under what circumstances would Ms. Adams be right?

Both sides can then be seen to be right. The next step is to see which of the two sets of circumstances most closely resembles the actual state of affairs.

The same approach can also be used in the evaluation of ideas by using the *best home* method. What would be the best home for this idea?

. . . This product would be wonderful for a large company with market dominance. This other product would be suitable for a small company trying to carve out a market niche. Well, which are we?

There are times when the blue hat thinker has to be quite blunt.

. . . We seem to have got stuck in an argument. We'll note both points of view and come back to it later.

. . . We are using the map mode and not the argument mode. If you have different points of view, just note them. Don't try to prove that yours is right and the other one is wrong.

. . . You have both had your say. To go any further is arguing and that is not what we are here to do.

. . . Will you please stop arguing.

. . . I want each of you to do some yellow hat thinking on the other person's point of view. That should stop the argument.

The formality of the blue hat allows any thinker to be much more direct than would otherwise be the case.

CHAPTER 47

Summary of Blue Hat Thinking

The blue hat is the control hat. The blue hat thinker organizes the thinking itself. Blue hat thinking is thinking about the thinking needed to explore the subject.

The blue hat thinker is like the conductor of the orchestra. The blue hat thinker calls for the use of the other hats.

The blue hat thinker defines the subjects towards which the thinking is to be directed. Blue hat thinking sets the focus. Blue hat thinking defines the problems and shapes the questions. Blue hat thinking determines the thinking tasks that are to be carried through.

Blue hat thinking is responsible for summaries, overviews and conclusions. These can take place from time to time in the course of the thinking and also at the end.

Blue hat thinking monitors the thinking and ensures that the rules of the game are observed. Blue hat thinking stops argument and insists on the map type of thinking. Blue hat thinking enforces the discipline.

195

Blue hat thinking may be used for occasional interjections which request a hat. Blue hat thinking may also be used to set up a step-by-step sequence of thinking operations which are to be followed just as a dance follows the choreography.

Even when the specific blue hat thinking role is assigned to one person, it is still open to anyone to offer blue hat comments and suggestions.

Conclusion

The biggest enemy of thinking is complexity, for that leads to confusion. When thinking is clear and simple, it becomes more enjoyable and more effective. The six thinking hats concept is very simple to understand. It is also very simple to use.

There are two main purposes to the six thinking hats concept. The first purpose is to simplify thinking by allowing a thinker to deal with one thing at a time. Instead of having to take care of emotions, logic, information, hope and creativity all at the same time, the thinker is able to deal with them separately. Instead of using logic to support a half-disguised emotion, the thinker can bring the emotion to the surface with the red thinking hat without any need to justify it. The black thinking hat can then deal with the logic aspect.

The second main purpose of the six thinking hats concept is to allow a *switch* in thinking. If a person at a meeting has been persistently negative, that person can be asked to take off "the black thinking hat." This signals to the person that he or she is being persistently negative. The person may also be asked to put on "the yellow thinking hat." This is a direct request to be positive. In this way the six hats provide an idiom that is definite without being offensive. What is most important is that the idiom does not threaten a

197

person's ego or personality. By turning it into role-playing or even a game, the concept of the hats makes it possible to request certain types of thinking. The hats become a sort of short-hand of instruction.

I am not suggesting that at every moment in our thinking we should consciously be using one hat or another. This is quite unnecessary. Occasionally we may want to go through the hats in a formal structured sequence and in such cases we would lay out the structure beforehand. More often we would want to put on one or other hat with some formality in the course of a discussion. Or we may want to request someone else at the discussion to put on a particular hat. At first this may seem a bit awkward but in time it will seem quite natural to make such a request.

It is obvious that the idiom will be most useful if all the people in an organization are aware of the rules of the game. For instance all those who are in the habit of meeting to discuss things should become aware of the meaning of the different hats. The concept works best when it has become a sort of common language.

Summaries
THE SIX THINKING HATS METHOD

The purpose of the six thinking hats is to unscramble thinking so that a thinker is able to use one thinking mode at a time – instead of trying to do everything at once. The best analogy is that of color printing. Each color is printed separately and in the end they all come together.

The six thinking hats method is designed to switch thinking away from the normal argument style to a mapmaking style. This makes thinking a two-stage process. The first stage is to make the map. The second stage is to choose a route on the map. If the map is good enough, the best route will often become obvious. As in the color printing analogy, each of the six hats puts one type of thinking on to the map.

I am not suggesting that the six hats cover every possible aspect of thinking, but they do cover the main modes. Nor am I suggesting that at every thinking moment we should be wearing one of the hats.

It is the very artificiality of the hats which is their greatest value. They provide a formality and a convenience for requesting a certain type of thinking either of oneself or of others. They establish rules for the game of thinking. Anyone playing the game will be aware of these rules.

199

The more the hats are used, the more they will become part of the thinking culture. Everyone in an organization should learn the basic idiom so that it can become part of the culture. This makes focused thinking much more powerful. Instead of wasting time in argument or drifting discussion, there will be a brisk and disciplined approach.

At first people might feel a little awkward about using the different hats, but this awkwardness soon passes as the convenience of the system becomes apparent. The first use of the hats will be in the form of an occasional request to use one hat or to switch from the black hat to another.

As I wrote at the beginning of the book, the great value of the hats is that they provide thinking roles. A thinker can take pride in playacting each of these roles. Without the formality of the hats, some thinkers would remain permanently stuck in one mode (usually the black hat mode).

I emphasize again that the system is a very easy one to use. There is no need for a reader to try to remember all the different points I have made in these pages. These points provide amplification. The essence of each hat is easy to remember.

White Hat virgin white, pure facts, figures and information.

Red Hat seeing red, emotions and feelings, also hunch and intuition.

Black Hat devil's advocate, negative judgement, why it will not work.

Yellow Hat sunshine, brightness and optimism, positive, constructive, opportunity.

Green Hat fertile, creative, plants springing from seeds, movement, provocation.

Blue Hat cool and control, orchestra conductor, thinking about thinking.

Within any organization the more people who learn the idiom the more usable it becomes. The truth is that we do not have a simple language as a control system for our thinking.

If we feel that we are intelligent enough to do without such a system, then we should consider that such a system would make that intelligence of which we are so proud even more effective. A person with natural running talent will benefit even more than others from discipline.

. . . At this point I want to make a yellow hat remark. Try it out for yourself.

For convenience I repeat on the following pages the summaries used in the book for each of the six thinking hats.

SUMMARY OF WHITE HAT THINKING

Imagine a computer that gives the facts and figures for which it is asked. The computer is neutral and objective. It does not offer interpretations or opinions. When wearing the white thinking hat, the thinker should imitate the computer.

The person requesting the information should use focusing questions in order to obtain information or information gaps.

In practice there is a two-tier system of information. The first tier contains checked and proven facts: first class facts. The second tier contains facts that are believed to be true but have not yet been fully checked: second class facts.

There is a spectrum of "likelihood" ranging from always true to never true. In between there are usable levels such as "by and large", "sometimes", and "occasional". Information of this sort can be put out under the white hat – provided the appropriate "frame" is used to indicate the likelihood.

White hat thinking is a discipline and a direction. The thinker strives to be more neutral and more objective in the presentation of information.

You can be asked to put on the white thinking hat or you can ask someone to put it on. You can also choose to put it on – or to take it off.

The white (absence of color) indicates neutrality.

SUMMARY OF RED HAT THINKING

Wearing the red hat allows the thinker to say: "This is how I feel about the matter."

The red hat legitimizes emotions and feelings as an important part of thinking.

The red hat makes feelings visible so that they can

become part of the thinking "map" and also part of the value system that chooses the route on the map.

The red hat provides a convenient method for a thinker to switch in and out of the "feeling" mode in a way that is not possible without such a device.

The red hat allows a thinker to explore the feelings of others by asking for a "red hat view".

When a thinker is using the red hat there should *never* be any attempt to justify the feelings or to provide a logical basis for them.

The red hat covers two broad types of feeling. Firstly, there are the ordinary emotions as we know them: ranging from the strong emotions such as fear and dislike to the more subtle ones such as suspicion. Secondly, there are the complex judgements that go into such types of "feeling" as hunch, intuition, sense, taste, aesthetic feeling and other not-visibly-justified types of feeling. Where an opinion has a large measure of this type of feeling it can also fit under the red hat.

SUMMARY OF BLACK HAT THINKING

Black hat thinking is specifically concerned with negative assessment. The black hat thinker points out what is wrong, incorrect and in error. The black hat thinker points out how something does not fit experience or accepted knowledge. The black hat thinker points out why something will not work. The black hat thinker points out risks and dangers. The black hat thinker points out faults in a design.

Black hat thinking is *not* argument and should never be

seen as such. It is an objective attempt to put the negative elements onto the map.

Black hat thinking may point out the errors in the thinking procedure and method itself.

Black hat thinking may judge an idea against the past to see how well it fits what is known.

Black hat thinking may project an idea into the future to see what might fail or go wrong.

Black hat thinking can ask "negative questions."

Black hat thinking should not be used to cover negative indulgence or negative feelings which should make use of the red hat.

Positive assessment is left for the yellow hat. In the case of new ideas the yellow hat should always be used before the black hat.

SUMMARY OF YELLOW HAT THINKING

Yellow hat thinking is positive and constructive. The yellow color symbolizes sunshine, brightness and optimism.

Yellow hat thinking is concerned with positive assessment just as black hat thinking is concerned with negative assessment.

Yellow hat thinking covers a positive spectrum that ranges from the logical and practical at one end to dreams, visions and hopes at the other end.

Yellow hat thinking probes and explores for value and benefit. Yellow hat thinking then strives to find logical support for this value and benefit. Yellow hat thinking seeks to put forward soundly based optimism but is not restricted to this – provided other types of optimism are appropriately labeled.

Yellow hat thinking is constructive and generative. It is from yellow hat thinking that come concrete proposals and suggestions. Yellow hat thinking is concerned with operacy and with "making things happen." Effectiveness is the aim of yellow hat constructive thinking.

Yellow hat thinking can be speculative and opportunity seeking. Yellow hat thinking also permits visions and dreams.

Yellow hat thinking is not concerned with mere positive euphoria (red hat) nor directly with creating new ideas (green hat).

SUMMARY OF GREEN HAT THINKING

The green hat is for creative thinking. The person who puts on the green hat is going to use the idioms of creative thinking. Those around are required to treat the output as a creative output. Ideally both thinker and listener should be wearing green hats.

The green color symbolizes fertility, growth and the value of seeds.

The search for alternatives is a fundamental aspect of green hat thinking. There is a need to go beyond the known and the obvious and the satisfactory.

With the creative pause the green hat thinker pauses at any point to consider whether there might be alternative ideas at that point. There need be no reason for this pause.

In green hat thinking the idiom of movement replaces that of judgement. The thinker seeks to move forward from an idea in order to reach a new idea.

Provocation is an important part of green hat thinking and is symbolized by the word *po*. A provocation is used to take us out of our usual patterns of thinking. There are many ways of setting up provocations including the random word method.

Lateral thinking is a set of attitudes, idioms and techniques (including movement, provocation and po) for cutting across patterns in a self-organizing asymmetric patterning system. It is used to generate new concepts and perceptions.

SUMMARY OF BLUE HAT THINKING

The blue hat is the "control" hat. The blue hat thinker organizes the thinking itself. Blue hat thinking is "thinking about the thinking needed to explore the subject."

The blue hat thinker is like the conductor of the orchestra. The blue hat thinker calls for the use of the other hats.

The blue hat thinker defines the subjects towards which the thinking is to be directed. Blue hat thinker sets the focus. Blue hat thinking defines the problems and shapes the questions. Blue hat thinking determines the thinking tasks that are to be carried through.

Blue hat thinking is responsible for summaries, over-, views and conclusions. These can take place from time to time in the course of the thinking, and also at the end.

Blue hat thinking monitors the thinking and ensures that the rules of the game are observed. Blue hat thinking stops argument and insists on the "map" type of thinking. Blue hat thinking enforces the discipline.

Blue hat thinking may be used for occasional interjections which request one or other hat. Blue hat thinking may also be used to set up a step by step sequence of thinking operations which are to be followed just as a dance follows the choreography.

Even when the specific blue hat thinking role is assigned to one person, it is still open to anyone to offer blue hat comments and suggestions.

EDWARD DE BONO

Publications mentioned in this book:

The Mechanism of Mind (Penguin Books)
Po: Beyond Yes and No (Penguin Books)
Lateral Thinking for Management (Penguin Books)
Lateral Thinking (Penguin Books, Harper & Row, NY)
Practical Thinking (Penguin Books)
Tactics: The Art and Science of Success (Little, Brown, NY)
Conflicts: A Better Way to Resolve Them (Harrap, UK)